Please return or renew this item before the latest date shown **below**

GLENWOOD 4/14

1 9 MAY 2014

2 2 OCT 2014

3 0 MAR 2016

- 8 SEP 2016

2 4 OCT 2016

31/10/16

10/1/17

ALSO BY ROBIN SIEGER

BOOKS
Silent Mind Golf
Silent Mind Putting
Natural Born Winners
You Can Change Your Life Anytime You Want
42 Days to Wealth, Health and Happiness
Passport to Success

AUDIO
Natural Born Winners
Pathway to Peace of Mind
Pathway to Success
NBW Guided Meditation

GOLF UNDER PRESSURE

Conquer the Choke Point with a Silent Mind

ROBIN SIEGER

Aurum
Press

First published in Great Britain
2012 by Aurum Press Ltd
74–77 White Lion Street
London N1 9PF
www.aurumpress.co.uk

This paperback edition first published in 2014 by Aurum Press Ltd

A catalogue record for this book is available from the British Library.

ISBN 978 1 78131 165 3

1 3 5 7 9 10 8 6 4 2
2014 2016 2018 2017 2015

Typeset by Saxon Graphics Ltd, Derby
Printed by CPI Group (UK) Ltd, Croydon, CR0 4YY

To
Matt Barr, Shaun Macdonald and
Mark Ritchie the other members of
my perfect fourball

CONTENTS

INTRODUCTION

Very few professional golfers ever win a major – and many never win a pro tournament. Yet, without exception, at some point in their career each has their chance. Even the long-time journeyman and no-hoper will, on one magical Sunday, find themselves in contention, their opportunity to win suddenly at hand. When that day comes they know it, the media know it and the spectators know it. What cannot be known – when that life-changing opportunity hinges on just one shot, the shot everyone knows will bring victory if successfully executed, the shot when the player has arrived at their personal 'moment of truth' – is the answer to the only question that matters: *can they do it?*

This moment is what they have dreamt about since they chose golf as their career. They have at last put themselves in a position to win; to do so they must play a critical shot, and execute it perfectly. However, this shot is unlike any other they have played before and as a consequence it takes on a completely new significance: it becomes a defining shot. Make it, they win; blow it and they will probably re-live it for years to come. The failure may become a monkey on their back the next time they come into contention, giving rise to unwelcome and unhelpful thoughts of self-doubt.

Golf, like life itself, is a pursuit in which many of the determining factors are played out within the lonely confines of the mind. And, clichéd as it may sound, life in turn really is like a game of golf, with the individual doing their best to handle the pressure, the setbacks and the disappointments, in the belief that in the end they will succeed. So when we have the opportunity to win and realise our aspiration, how do we make sure we do not blow it?

Is it something we are born with? Is it the result of a strong mind and immense self-belief? Is it something we can learn, something we can prepare for? Curiously this was a question I found myself pondering after reading a book on military history on a long journey.

In the Second World War, many ordinary members of the public with no military training were conscripted into the armed forces; others volunteered. I became interested in those who not only volunteered (willingly signing up despite the risk of death or injury), but then, once in the services, volunteered again for elite units, with their demanding standards of acceptance and even greater risk of death.

Whilst reading about the early formation of the airborne forces, what really caught my attention was the testimony of a former training instructor of young paratroopers. He recalled that in training there were some stand-out guys, who were fit, motivated, tough as old boots and natural warriors, and there were others, always at the back on the training runs or speed marches, who were anything but natural, were far from the best soldiers, got reprimanded more than others and were often close to being kicked out. The instructors instinctively assumed that when they went into combat the guys who were great in training would be good in action. However, this assumption was repeatedly proven to be false. Often it was the quiet guy, who had been average in training and hadn't stood out, who ended up leading the charge. And in some cases the guy you would have bet your life on, the 'natural warrior' in training, simply froze. This was of course a generalisation, but the notion that, irrespective of what training suggested, you really couldn't predict who would rise to the challenge and who would be overwhelmed by it is a striking one.

It is a recurring theme in accounts of warfare that the soldiers' greatest unknown, their greatest fear, was how they would perform when the bullets were real. This horrific baptism of fire would be life or death, not a game or training exercise. Nowhere is the notion that a point in time can provide a dramatic moment of truth, where the individual will either freeze or fight, more apparent.

This ultimate test on the battlefield, I felt, had some clear parallels with people facing their own 'moments of truth'. And my natural inclination was to look for the golfing moment of truth, and try to understand it. But it seemed to me that a better approach to consider than 'freeze or fight' was 'lose control or take control'. I wanted to study those players who had lost control and those who had taken control; how they managed it, or didn't. I was convinced that these insights would go some way to unlocking the mystery of those who perform under pressure and those who 'choke'.

To find our cure we need to be aware of the causes. My primary purpose in writing this book has been to offer some reflections and guidance on the *why* and the *what* of choking under pressure. Why do we choke? And what can we do about it? Some of the chapters that follow explore ways in which we can understand the sequence of thoughts and reactions that prevent us from playing at our best. Other chapters will set out specific strategies, instructions and exercises to help us conquer the 'choke point' and play that crucial shot.

When I wrote *Silent Mind Golf* I described what I believe to be the best possible mental state we need to be in to play our best golf, and what we can do to get ourselves into that state of mind. However, I received the same feedback again and again. Although the Silent Mind approach makes perfect sense, and works on the practice ground, out on the course, in competition, it is much harder to apply, especially at those crucial moments when it is most needed. Pressure was the elephant in the room, and though I had touched on it in my first book, I realised I had to take a closer look at how we might master the pressure shots; the shots that determine who wins and who loses.

There are always factors that are beyond our control. What is within our control is how we train ourselves to react. In that realisation, I believe, lies the key to unlocking the mystery of how to take control when under pressure – the key to facing our own moment of truth on the course.

1
THE CHOKE

**'Relax? How can anybody relax
and play golf?'**

Ben Hogan

The history of sport is full of iconic individuals whose winning actions under the greatest imaginable pressure define them forever. Irrespective of what else they go on to do in life, their greatest success remains a moment frozen in time, etched into the memories of those who witnessed it – the stuff of legend. Such moments are remembered not only for the victory that ensued, but because we know that when those sporting giants were faced with hitting the perfect shot under massive pressure, their nerve didn't let them down. They held it together. They didn't choke.

Equally, there are players whose careers have never recovered from the agony of a failure snatched from the jaws of victory: when their first opportunity to win a professional tournament appeared, they stumbled, and irrespective of the reasons they later offered up, deep in their hearts they know they choked. Some recover from failure and others don't. Until we experience an on-course meltdown, its reality – and consequences – can only be imagined.

Choking is not the preserve of professional athletes or golfers. Each of us can succumb to pressure, at work as well as on the golf course. It is never an enjoyable experience, and more often than not it is the anticipation rather than the actual execution that is the cause of our anguish. I am sure we would all like to exhibit the super-cool, calm-under-pressure persona of those characters we so often see in movies, who, when the odds are stacked against them, walk out to face their nemeses without a bead of sweat on their foreheads, certain they will succeed – and invariably do so. But life is not like the movies. When we are in a match and we have to hit a soft lob from a tight lie over a bunker to pin cut just on the green, I doubt there are many of us who don't experience self-imposed pressure, as we momentarily think about the multitude of hazards and things that might go wrong.

Yet these are the shots we live for; these are the shots that define us as the players we believe we are, or wish to be. Golf would become a very boring sport if every shot were simple and straightforward, if we were not truly tested and challenged. However, the same challenge faces us when the shot is simple but the pressure is on. The stakes of these shots can be so immense that a perfect execution results in an emotional high – whilst a mis-hit brings toe-curling, buttock-clenching agony.

I am sure you've seen the photographs of players who have just missed a short putt or sent a wedge a few feet short to land in the creek. The cold hard truth of despair is clear from their body language. Some drop their heads and some just gaze blankly, unable to believe what they have just seen and done. The shaking of the head, the dropping of the shoulders, the look of injustice and disbelief: this is the agony of golf in its most naked form.

Golf is not a fair game; it never has been. What makes it so compelling, however, is the ability of an individual to manage the pressure, to take the good and the bad with equal grace, to accept the luck of the bounce and never lose their belief in playing their best, whatever the situation. This is the ideal to which we must aspire if we are going to be a master of our game under pressure: to be calm, confident and in control; to be a player who, when the chips are down, stands firm and simply does not choke.

This is all fine in theory, but one would need the emotional absence of a robot to feel nothing at all when under pressure. Whether we are standing on the 18th tee knowing we need a par to score our best round ever, or standing on the 72nd tee of a major needing par to win, the pressure builds the closer we come to winning. Indeed, pressure is a crucial part of the game and gets our competitive juices flowing. **There is no point trying to ignore that pressure; what we need to do is create strategies to manage it**, rather than allowing it to master us.

A person who is afraid of flying gets progressively more anxious the closer they get to an unavoidable flight. This is because the things we fear we tend to fixate on. So, if we have a fear of choking, we will put more stress upon ourselves when we find ourselves in a high-pressure situation, where choking is a possibility. But the key is: do not be afraid of choking. It might be surprising to read these words here, but I believe that if we do not *fear* choking we will be less likely to *fixate* on choking when out on the course – and less likely to *fulfil* the act of choking when faced with a critical shot. We must admit that choking can happen, but prevent this reality from causing us fear. The fear of choking should have no place in our thought process. We should plan and prepare for the best, and when we do choke under pressure, rather than beat ourselves up or get mad, we should look at what went wrong, learn from it and seek to fix it – rather than label ourselves a 'choker'.

Jack Nicklaus said about pressure, 'You just hope you have enough chances to experience it, and get used to it.' So it is best that **we learn from the pressure situations and, over time, become more comfortable with pressure, building up our pressure threshold, in a sense, building up our tolerance.** This does not mean the pressure will go away – it won't, as long as winning matters. But it does mean that, just as a person at the gym, through repeated practice, is able to increase the amount of weight they can lift, so we too can train ourselves to play golf successfully under increased levels of pressure.

> **There is no point trying to ignore the pressure. What we need to do is create strategies to manage it.**

2

THE CHOKE POINT

'Everyone has his own choking level, a level at which he fails to play his normal golf. As you get more experienced, your choking level rises.'

Johnny Miller

I have read too many biographies of great golfers and accounts of matches to believe there has been anyone in the history of the game who has not choked. It's just a matter of where and when. Everyone has a pressure limit and once that limit is reached their game is almost certain to be disturbed, from a slight loss of timing to a complete mishit. In the professional game, some players can put a bad shot in context and move on, whilst others remain haunted by it for the rest of their lives, some to such an extent that they eventually give up the game. They have lost all confidence in their own ability to compete, and no longer believe their game will hold up under pressure.

Those golfers who are noted for being good pressure players generally come from competitive backgrounds. It seems to be a product of their childhood environment. Some grow up in hardship, having to compete both inside and outside the family to succeed. Other individuals are just born with a highly competitive streak, and seek to win at everything they do. Their will to win is overwhelming; with such players it is difficult to have a friendly game of dominoes or cards, or even walk up a hill, without winning or coming first being their aim.

To play our best golf under pressure we need to know where our choke point lies. That is, the level of pressure we can manage before our game gives way or becomes unreliable. When I was studying at university I met a fellow who studied metallurgy, and in particular the tensile strengths of different types of steel, to measure the point at which samples would fracture due to the pressure exerted upon them becoming too great. In science, and in life generally, there are stresses that can be managed, and others that cause a breakdown. In the case of steel, the fewer impurities, the higher its strength. So the aim of the metallurgist when seeking to increase the tensile strength of steel is to rid it of impurities.

As golfers, we have a comfort zone in which we play our most relaxed (and generally our best) golf. But when we are in competition and the pressure builds, we will eventually reach our own choke point. We need to understand where it is and create strategies to allow ourselves to stay calm at that level of stress. Then, those situations that previously would have caused us to become sweaty-palmed and anxious will no longer do so, as we have learnt to manage them.

What we cannot do is create conditions where we simply don't feel pressure: that would be impossible. Instead, **we need to build up our tolerance to pressure and rid ourselves of those mental impurities that create unwanted pressure**, allowing us to manage the pressure in a way that enables us to retain control.

A simple analogy would be for you to get in a Formula One racing car and drive it as fast as possible around a racetrack. You would certainly find it an exhilarating experience. I have no doubt you would be sufficiently cautious not to spin off the road and kill yourself. But if, upon finishing your first lap, you were told you were over 80 seconds slower than the slowest Formula One driver on this racetrack circuit, and then asked if you would like to try again, to make it round a bit faster, you might now put yourself under pressure, and feel less comfortable and confident as a result. This would mean going faster on the straights and going around corners at a slightly higher speed, thus increasing the risk of spinning off the road. It would be a nervy affair at best, and you may or may not be a few seconds faster. However, if you were then to spend three weeks under the guidance of a professional race drive instructor, your capacity to deal with the pressure would increase as your technical ability increased, and you would have more confidence in the car and your own skill. You would thereby raise the choke point – the point at which you become too stressed to be effective.

The same is true of golf. When Tom Watson said you have to learn how to lose before you learn how to win, he was identifying the conditions we require to develop a stronger mental game. Winning is a state of mind; **those who are able to win consistently have better mental discipline and the priceless ability to control their fear when under pressure.** When, as has often happened, winners lose that ability, it generally marks the end of their careers. It is the rare individual who overcomes this setback and returns once again to the winner's circle.

I believe that everybody feels pressure and, as a result, everyone has a choke point. Anyone who says they don't choke or don't feel the pressure either has not reached their choke point in their game, or is in denial (I would suggest the latter). It is our position on the pressure spectrum that determines how we play under duress: the ability to deal with pressure, or compartmentalise it in the mind, separates those who perform well under pressure and those who don't.

If we look at people who participate in extreme sports, we find that they have all built up their mental capacity to manage the pressure through gradual exposure, thereby enabling them to perform at their very best when it matters. They are without doubt thrill-seekers, but they have no death wish. In fact, if you ever ask about their particular activity, you find them to be highly safety-conscious.

BASE jumping is a branch of parachuting in which individuals jump off a fixed object – Building, Antenna, Span (bridge) or Earth (cliff or similar) – with only one parachute, which they open when close to the ground (they have no reserve parachute). Within the BASE jumping community, there is a small group of people who jump off cliffs wearing wing suits which allow them to enjoy a much longer glide through the air; as a consequence they have much more control over their direction than regular jumpers. In the early days of the sport people with wing suits would jump off a cliff and get as far away from it as possible, as it represented a hazard. In recent years, however, a new group of jumpers has emerged called 'proximity flyers', who, once they have jumped off the cliff, fly back towards it, then parallel to it, getting as close to the cliff face as they can. They also follow the contour of the ground, sometimes clearing obstacles by less than ten feet. The margin of error is tiny. Any contact with a stationary object will almost certainly kill them. I suspect when it comes to pressure in sport, nothing beats that faced by the proximity flyers. Any 'choke' could result in almost certain death, especially when flying so close to the edge of safety.

Despite the very different physical risk, golfers can learn a lot from the BASE jumping skydivers, who not only demonstrate the importance of a desire to achieve, but also illustrate the importance of training oneself to manage physical action whilst under the greatest mental pressure. They visualise the jump, they run through it in their minds a number of times and, as the old adage goes, in the world of skydiving *they plan their jump and they jump their plan.*

Too often in golf, when we find ourselves in a high-pressure situation, the only thing we recognise is the emotional feeling, and

we neglect the shot. The shot becomes a secondary issue as we fight to control our increasing heart rate or negative self-talk. To manage pressure successfully, like the BASE jumper, we need to visualise exactly the scenario we are going to face and execute a routine or a plan we have already mentally rehearsed.

Pressure in golf is compulsory; it goes with the territory. Much as we would like to play competition golf with the immense calm of a Zen monk, in reality it is almost impossible. We are not creatures of logic, but rather creatures of emotion. We will never be able to become devoid of emotion – or pressure. What we can do is learn how to manage it and, to a much greater extent than we might imagine, raise our capacity to deal with it.

> **Pressure is unavoidable;**
> **choking is optional.**

3

THE FEAR FACTOR

**'The person I fear most in the last
two rounds is myself.'**

Tom Watson

Why does pressure cause us to choke? **We choke and become emotionally overloaded when under pressure, because we are afraid of something going wrong** – something that is our own fault. When we become fearful we fail to operate intuitively, we refuse to allow our physical actions to flow in the involuntary manner they have been trained through practice and experience. At such moments we deliberately become very aware of everything around us, and in this state of heightened awareness we become fully self-conscious. This can lead us to get irritated by the smallest thing. As the writer P.G. Wodehouse expressed so succinctly in his short story 'Ordeal by Golf', 'The least thing upset him on the links. He missed short putts because of the uproar of butterflies in the adjoining meadow.'

When we become fearful or stressed, our body releases adrenalin into the blood and this adrenalin causes the heart to beat faster and prepares the body to fight or to run. But there is a third option for those who don't opt to fight or run: they simply freeze. Many golfers will tell you that when they have been under pressure and nervous they have become very self-aware as a result. They could hear their heart beating. They momentarily stopped breathing. This is what we do as children when we are afraid at night. When we are lying in bed and suddenly hear a noise that gives us a fright, we can hear our little hearts thumping in our chests as our ears become super-attuned to the slightest noise in our immediate environment. These are the effects of adrenalin – and they allow us to become distracted. Some professional golfers betray their distraction by asking near-silent galleries to be quiet, or by becoming preoccupied with simple things that in a normal round would not concern them.

In the Ryder Cup at Oak Hill Country Club in 1995, Nick Faldo, having played a superb wedge at the final par-four hole, had a four-foot putt to give himself a chance of beating Curtis Strange and winning the tournament for Europe. To the spectator watching on television it was business as usual and we knew that if anyone in that situation was capable of making that putt it was Nick Faldo. He stroked the putt dead into the centre of the cup. When interviewed afterwards, however, he admitted he had been physically shaking and his heart had been thumping; he really didn't know how he had got the club back. I suspect that no matter how much Faldo understood the physiological process of choking, given the amount of pressure on that putt, it would have been almost impossible for him to be casual about it. The important thing was that when the pressure came he *was* able to function, he was not overcome, he did not panic, he did not freeze. He did not choke. He was able to swing the putter smoothly enough to make the shot, even though he had so much adrenalin coursing through his body that, by his own admission, he could feel himself shaking.

Other players in that situation could so easily have pushed or pulled the putt badly, losing control over the delicate muscle motor skills required for such a shot. Rather than playing the shot as they would during a regular session on the range, when a player chokes it is often because they become emotionally overloaded with the negative potential consequences of the action before them. Just as some players are afraid of losing, others are distracted by winning, because both of those outcomes have a high emotional value and inevitably create tension.

When Doug Sanders stood over the infamous putt he needed to win the Open Championship at St Andrews in 1970, he was already thinking about what to do after he holed the winning putt. Explaining his thought process in a subsequent interview, he wondered: should he raise his hands into the air?, or do something else appropriate to that moment? He had got ahead of himself and, while his thoughts might be seen as positive, in practice they distracted him and created a heightened awareness of the implications of the putt, thereby unconsciously raising the stress and so the difficulty of the shot at hand.

There are players who have won majors through the accomplishment of astonishing shots. Two of the most famous of all time have been Larry Mize's once-in-a-lifetime chip during the sudden-death play-off of the 1987 US Masters against Greg Norman, and Bob Tway's holed bunker shot on the final hole of the 1986 USPGA Championship (also ironically against Greg Norman). Both bordered on the unbelievable. I doubt any bookmaker would have given you odds shorter than 1000 to one on either player achieving those shots. And I believe that because of the extreme difficulty they faced, neither player realistically thought they would make the shot. As a result, I believe they were not especially anxious or emotionally overloaded as they stood over the ball, and this physical and mental state put them in the best possible position to hit it perfectly – which is exactly what they did.

Fear of losing is a much stronger emotion than fear of winning. This is one reason more tournaments are won by the players who are not leading at the start of the final round: they have no position to protect. So, is there anything we can do to reduce our fear? When I took up skydiving some years ago, I remember being very nervous about the whole jump sequence. From the moment I gave my name to the flight manifester and was told which load I would be boarding, right up until when I exited the plane, I had an uneasy tension in my stomach, like a million butterflies having a party. Curiously when I left the aircraft at 12,500 feet the fear and anxiety went away. Why? I believe that once out of the aircraft and in freefall I was 'in the moment': I had no time to process the future, so wholly engaged was I with the here and now.

After I had accumulated over 120 jumps, I realised I still got fairly nervous before each jump. True, the sensation was a little less intense, but it remained and it was unpleasant. I had thought that with experience my confidence would grow and these 'jitters' would disappear. I discussed it with a number of more experienced skydivers and instructors, and they told me that the fear never really goes away. Even those with over 8000 jumps told me they still got a little nervous before each jump!

Pressure never goes away, but by learning to accept it as part of the process and enjoyment of the sport you love, **you will get used to it.** When we play golf under pressure, we will experience emotions that are similar to fear or worry. If we simply try to ignore them, I doubt we will have much success – the processes at work are too central to our physiology. Better that we learn from the skydivers who come to accept that it is normal and natural to experience fear. Through rehearsing the negative scenarios that could happen and practising their emergency drills as normal, the skydivers are able to *manage* any potential situation. As golfers we have to do the same, and not let situations overwhelm us, which is what is happening when we choke.

DEFUSE THE STRESS ▶

1 Sit upright in a chair, close your eyes and breathe slowly and deeply. Do this for about two minutes all the time consciously relaxing your body on the exhale.

2 Now, visualise yourself facing a stressful shot on the golf course, a shot that historically you have not played well – a shot that if you faced it on the course would create tension.

3 Have a clear sense of this shot and the associated thoughts and emotions.

4 When you have done this, continue breathing slowly and deeply, and let go of any negative thoughts and emotions. With each breath 'see' yourself with positive body language, 'feel' yourself confident, 'tell' yourself this shot is 'no big deal'.

5 Now visualise yourself playing the shot perfectly.

6 Be aware of the positive thoughts, feelings and emotions that this image creates.

7 Repeat the visualised perfect shot with the positive thoughts and emotions.

8 After ten minutes spend a few moments slowly returning to full awareness in the chair.

The purpose of this exercise is to familiarise yourself with the 'experience' of playing well under pressure. By creating a 'false' memory of success under pressure, you will be able to 'recall' playing well when in a real situation.

Just as the skydiver rehearses on the ground what they will do in the air during an emergency, golfers need to rehearse mentally, off the course, what they will do in a pressure situation on it. The more we do this, the deeper in our subconscious will we embed the memory of managing pressure on the course. When we find ourselves in competition for real, and face a pressure shot that we have visualised a hundred times or more, we will have the memory of having hit the shot just the way we want.

Fear of losing is a stronger emotion than fear of winning, so focus your expectation on a successful outcome. Accentuate the positive.

4
GETTING TO THE COMFORT ZONE

'The less tension and effort, the faster and more powerful you will be.'

Bruce Lee

I am not a fan of the word 'choke'. It is used to suggest weakness, implying a person is inadequate or incapable of performing a skill that, when not under pressure, they can perform effortlessly. It is slang, and is usually uttered by the professional or amateur critic who has never been in the cauldron of top-flight sporting pressure, and whose own actions will never be examined under the unforgiving spotlight of the viewing public. I prefer to think of choking as 'emotional overload'. Because that is exactly what it is.

Early in his career, Tom Watson was branded a choker. Yet when he won the 1975 Open Championship in Carnoustie in a play-off against Jack Newton, he said that before you can learn to win you have to learn to lose. There is another way to look at this: **success is learned through a process of wisdom, experience and knowledge that finds its origins in past failure.** In fact, according to those who research motion in child development, failure is essential to success. The average child falls over 240 times while learning to walk. The falling over is simply (in scientific terms) biofeedback, allowing the child's balance and motor learning centres to calibrate the body position required to stay upright and walk without toppling over. The same can be seen when we learn to speak, dress ourselves, swim or ride a bike. Our whole experience of success in life comes after a series of related failures.

Therefore, when Tom Watson acknowledged that victory comes after repeated losses he was stating a fact that is often overlooked. **We learn to succeed through a process of failure.** Yet once we have learned to succeed we should be able to use that experience to build our confidence to a point where we are able to perform established routines with ease. In theory, when we are under pressure we should enter into, and remain in, our 'comfort zone', where we are relaxed and calm. But, as we know, this simply is not the way golf – or life – plays out.

Here's a very simple example to illustrate the point. If we were to ask someone to walk along a plank ten inches wide and fourteen feet long whilst it is lying on the floor, this would probably strike that person as a very easy task and more than likely they would perform it with ease and confidence. However, if we then raised the plank a hundred feet off the ground and put it between two brick walls, our proposition would seem very different, as the risk factor would have increased way beyond most people's comfort zone. But what if we asked an experienced high-wire tightrope walker? How would they cope? Surely, with ease, as they would still be well within their comfort zone. So handling pressure is best managed by those who, through either experience or other learning, have expanded their comfort zone, and no longer experience the emotional overload they would previously have suffered.

When we witness a professional sportsman being overcome by pressure there is, I imagine, universal empathy with the plight of the player at that moment. However, I doubt there is much any of us could say that would bring comfort or make a difference. Well-intentioned comments such as 'Calm down,' 'Take a deep breath,'

'Slow down,' or a dramatic attempt at reverse psychology such as 'Pull yourself together,' would not make much difference to the player. The reason is that the player is outside their comfort zone, and experiencing fear. **If you don't have a coping strategy to manage pressure when you experience it for real, trust me, you are not magically going to find it on the course in the heat of battle.**

My brother-in-law is a doctor and has always been able to explain complex medical matters to me in a manner I am able to understand. I asked him one day to explain the step-by-step process of a heart attack. I don't remember why I asked – though coming from the west coast of Scotland, which has the highest rates of heart disease in the world, may have had something to do with it! Paul proceeded to explain in detail the stages of a heart attack, and though it became clear that a healthy diet, lifestyle and exercise programme would greatly reduce the probability of my suffering a heart attack, this knowledge did not for a moment mean that I was now able to avoid having one. What it gave me was clear strategies to reduce the chances.

This is equally true of the experience of choking under pressure – of experiencing the full force of emotional overload. Even though we can explore step-by-step the causes of choking, both psychologically through analysis of the thought process, and physiologically through consideration of the effects of adrenalin on the body, it does not mean that when the moment arrives we will not choke, or indeed that we are less likely to. When under pressure, the knowledge of how choking works will be just that – knowledge – not a magic spell to stop it happening. What this knowledge does give us is a chance to create a strategy to avoid falling prey to the meltdown.

Do not mistake knowledge for ability. There is nothing truly complicated about the mental side of the game; most of what I describe in this book has been known for over a hundred years. Equally, the golf swing has not changed too much over the past 70 years, yet thousands of books have been written about the swing, and people still invest in these books, not to mention training aids, instruction and technology in the hope of mastering their own swing and learning the lessons required to play great golf. In truth very few ever do. They are making the mistake of thinking that because they *know* what to do, this means they *can* do it. This is the theory–practice gap: I understand what I need to do, I just don't have the ability to do it. It is for this reason that as golfers we cannot just learn the lessons of the game; we must also invest time in practice both on and – equally importantly – off the course.

SAFE PLACE ▶

When we are young children there are places we go to when we want to feel safe. Normally it is our parents' arms, but it can be our bedrooms or any other location we associate with safety and security. As we get older and life gets more frantic, we often substitute unhealthy lifestyle choices to give ourselves these feelings, most notably alcohol, drugs, smoking, and over-eating. This exercise is a great way to experience healthy 'safe' feelings any time, any place, and the more you do it the more permanently established in your life those feelings will become.

1 Sit down in a chair with your legs uncrossed, keeping your back reasonably upright; it is key that you do not slouch, or get into a position from which you can fall asleep. The important thing is to sit in a relaxed manner, your feet planted on the floor. At this point, your hands may be gently resting on top of your legs or loosely clasped together.

2 Consciously begin to breathe in deeply and breathe out slowly. After ten or twelve deep breaths just focus on your breathing – breathe in, breathe out – and as you exhale consciously relax your body.

SAFE PLACE (*continued*) ▶

3 I want you to visualise that you are at a place where you are very happy, and feel safe and secure. It can be a real place you have visited in your life, or it can be an imagined place that you have always dreamed of going to. The important thing is that it is a place where you feel safe and relaxed.

4 If thoughts drift into your mind, do not dwell on them but let them flow away again by bringing your attention back to your breathing.

5 Stay focused on feeling safe, confident and calm.

6 After ten to fifteen minutes spend a few moments slowly returning to full awareness in the chair.

The purpose of this exercise is to enable you to experience feelings of security and deep relaxation. If you can do this regularly, the feeling of confidence produced will continue throughout the day.

The more they practise this visualisation exercise, the more they embed the memory of it in their subconscious mind, and the more normal it feels. Nerves will no longer be a dominant concern, as through repeated practice the subject will create a memory, albeit imagined, of themselves relaxed and calm on the course.

Few people practise such exercises; they think understanding the concept means they can do it. But to play better golf under pressure we need to commit to spending time every day (ten minutes will be plenty) engaging in positive mental visualisations of the scenarios which in the past have caused us to tense up.

Learning to be relaxed under pressure
comes through repeated experience of
playing under pressure – both real and
imagined.

5

BREAK THE CHAIN

'If there is doubt in your mind, how can your muscles know what they are expected to do?'

Harvey Penick

When a player chokes over a simple shot they would routinely make in practice, we assume it is because the pressure they were under impeded their ability to execute the critical shot.

It is my experience that when a player finds himself under great pressure over a shot, it is not a sudden event; rather it results from the gradual build-up of stress over the preceding hours and in some cases even days. Pressure grows through a chain of events. Each one taken on its own would be manageable, but when these little events accumulate, the pressure can become too much to handle All competitive sports people experience stress; it goes with competition. However, **stress rarely just disappears; it accumulates and hangs around in our minds, so given enough time a little constant stress will become big stress.**

We need to learn to break the chain that allows the pressure to build. Let me give you an example. Imagine you're sitting in a room and have one hour to read a document in detail before answering questions on it in a short test that same day. Outside, on a nearby building site, is a mechanical piledriver which every twelve seconds makes a dull clunking noise, not a loud sound but loud enough that you are aware of it. You sit down but pay no attention to this distant sound because why should you? It really doesn't bother you, because you are quite rightly concentrating on the document you have only an hour to read.

After ten minutes the noise has now entered your consciousness and you are finding it increasingly difficult to concentrate on reading and comprehending the document. After twenty minutes you're annoyed, indeed you may well be angry, because you can't concentrate on the document because of that darned clunking noise going on in the street outside. After another five minutes you're unable to continue reading the document because the noise outside has made it impossible for you to study. Ultimately you give up, or complain that you cannot study under such conditions.

This is not dissimilar to what happens to golfers in competition. Instead of the audible clunk of a piledrive, we have to contend with a steady stream of negative thoughts and worries making us concerned about how we will handle pressure when it comes. By allowing the pressure to build, we inadvertently sabotage our own technique – in a sense, we create the perfect storm that, when the pressure is sufficiently high, will allow us readily to choke.

The more we can delay the chain of events that allows pressure to build, the better. Let's go back to the room with the piledriver outside making the dull noise. We need to find a way to negate the impact of this noise. The most obvious way is to go to a different room, but that is not always possible. The other solution is to direct our attention away from the noise and back to the book. Though we will still be aware of the noise, we will choose to let it 'flow over us', and not to focus on it, or allow ourselves to get upset about it. Instead we will look for ways to lessen the sound by closing a window or even putting earplugs or cotton wool in our ears to muffle it. Silly as this might seem, we must always look for solutions that enable us to stay as relaxed as possible.

On the golf course the same dynamic arises: we start to worry about an aspect of our game that is not working and it creeps into our thoughts. **When negative thoughts begin to flow** – 'Don't hit a slice,' 'Don't three-putt,' 'Keep it out the bunker' – **we need to shut them out.** We must not pay attention to such thoughts, because that is all they are – thoughts – and the only value they have is the value we attribute to them. **An excellent approach to negative thoughts when they arise is to let them flow over us: don't pay attention to them**; don't waste time trying to rationalise them; don't imagine them to be psychic predictions for the future. They are merely negative thoughts that we simply should not focus on.

This is easier when we can think positively about shots we have played in the past, and simply recall the good feelings and memories we associate with them. One of the important roles of a professional caddy is to know when their player is going into a bit of a mental slump, or getting too tense. They will talk about mundane things to distract their player from 'over-thinking' their game and to help them relax a little. Many caddies will deliberately walk more slowly and encourage their players to walk at the same pace, because when we tense up we speed up; slowing down will help to reduce tension.

Winning is important. I say this in case it appears I am advocating a languid approach on the course, not keeping score, valuing the exercise, simply enjoying yourself with a 'Hey! It's only a game after all, and nobody died' attitude. I play to win every time I tee it up, and so do the vast majority of people I know who play golf. And since winning is important, especially in the professional game, we need to think about any aspect of our form which is weak and requires attention. **Managing negative thoughts is a key area for most players**.

To get ourselves in the optimal mindset to play well, we need to be relaxed but aware, and not let the pressure build too quickly and grow out of control.

If we consciously break the chain of negative thinking that allows pressure to build, we will begin to create the positive mindset to play better golf.

6

EVERYONE FEELS THE PRESSURE

'Anyone who hasn't been nervous, or who hasn't choked somewhere down the line, is an idiot.'

Cary Middlecroft

The top tour professionals in the world feel the heat of pressure, just like you and me. Never imagine that because they play the game for a living, the game's household names are immune to pressure. The main difference is that these players have been in pressure situations so many times in their careers that through repeated exposure they have (usually) become much better at coping with it.

Stage performers who every night walk out in front of a new audience to perform and entertain confess to experiencing nerves before they go onstage. Once in front of the audience, however, there is no time for them to worry about what is happening, as they are 'in the moment', delivering their performance.

Clients I have worked with who have a history of choking under pressure, be it in a job interview or in contention in a golf tournament, almost without exception state they succumbed to the pressure because they became too self-aware and started overanalysing – both themselves and the things that could go wrong. Some start running worst-case scenarios in their head ('What's the worst thing that could happen here?'), and then fixating on them. They then try to control everything they do and in the process lose confidence.

The ideal state to be in is 'unconscious excellence'. In this state we act or perform without thinking. We experience this state when we do something we have done hundreds of times before. When we walk around our home we don't think of the actions required to do so; these are familiar and have become automatic. Likewise, the more professionals play under pressure, the more used to it they become, and the better able they are to manage it.

The worst state to be in is 'conscious trying', which arises when players become too self-aware. Rather than acting naturally and confidently we become stiff, unnatural and uncertain, completely at odds with the automatic actions of performing without thinking.

There are two schools of thought regarding an individual's ability to manage extreme pressure. Some think we are born with a capacity to manage pressure; others believe not. The first view is pretty pessimistic: if we're not born with it, then the capacity to manage pressure will forever elude us, as we can never acquire it. Indeed, there have been immensely talented golfers who never won a major and never realised their full potential. When the question is asked why not, the answer often ventured is that they couldn't handle the pressure. It is a harsh burden for many golfers to bear, that in the eyes of their peers or fans, despite their talent, they were never good enough to win the big ones, and somehow no matter how close they come they will never succeed. But is this because they were born without that magic ingredient – the ability to manage pressure?

I believe there are individuals who are born with a calm and confident disposition, just as there are people who are born with an uptight and nervous disposition. Nevertheless, I contend that the person who was born with an uptight and nervous disposition can, through time and dedicated practice, train themselves to be more relaxed. I also believe that neither personality type will indicate with any certainty which of the individuals will go on to be a champion (think back to the example of the paratroopers and their performance in training versus battle). At the extremes of these personality types, there are those who are too laid back ever to win, and others who are just too uptight, but these are the very rare exceptions. In the final analysis, it is the players who have learned to master themselves and their own fears in the heat of battle that become the champions.

The 1977 Open Championship was played in Turnberry, Scotland. For the last fifteen years, 37-year-old Jack Nicklaus had dominated the professional game. Then, in that year's Masters, having been tied for the lead with four holes to play, he lost by two shots.

The man who beat him was Tom Watson, who at 27 years of age was the pretender to the throne. Watson was an immensely talented golfer who early in his career had been labelled a choker. In the 1974 US Open he had led after 36 holes but hit a 79 in the final round to finish five shots behind the winner. A year later, after excellent opening rounds, he once again faded away. He sought guidance from US golfing legend Byron Nelson, five-time major champion, winner of eleven consecutive PGA tournaments in 1945 and 'father of the modern swing'. The two of them began working together on Watson's game.

Going into the Open Championship at Carnoustie in 1975, Watson asked Nelson how to react to the inevitable problems of wind and rain. Nelson's advice is probably best summarised as 'Don't worry.' He pointed out to Watson that everyone else would be facing the same problems. After so many near misses, Watson won his first major that year.

In 1977 at the Open Championship Watson and Nicklaus played, by any measure, the most outstanding golf seen in a major. They went head-to-head like two heavyweight boxers trading blows, with a barrage of birdies and magnificent shot-making under pressure. They were so far ahead of the field that it seemed everyone else was in another tournament. After 72 holes, they were ten shots clear of

Hubert Green in third place. Such was the drama and intensity of their encounter that it became known as the 'Duel in the Sun'. If you have not read the story of this titanic encounter, I would encourage you to do so, as it is as dramatic and inspirational a game of golf as we're ever likely to see again. Much as I would love to give you a blow-by-blow account of Watson and Nicklaus's battle here, there is just one small aspect that I wish to highlight.

Early in the final round Nicklaus opened a two-shot lead over Watson. Lesser mortals might have seen this as an inevitable charge with which there would be no catching up. But Watson truly believed he was going to win and did not lose heart or give up. He fought back with birdies. At the sixteenth hole, a par-three, Watson pulled his drive slightly and his ball landed off the green in light rough. Nicklaus played a good five-iron leaving himself a birdie putt. The advantage was clearly with Nicklaus, but Watson then did the seemingly impossible. He rolled his sixty-foot putt from the fringe of the green straight into the hole. Nicklaus missed his birdie putt and after 69 holes the two players were tied for the lead.

It is difficult to imagine the pressure on both these players, both wonderful golfers and keen competitors, in part because they handled it so magnificently. As they stood on the sixteenth tee waiting to play, Watson turned to Nicklaus and said, 'This is what it's all about, isn't it?' Nicklaus smiled at Watson and said, 'You bet it is.'

At the point in the competition when most people would be tight or very intensely focused, these two players were able to enter into a dialogue that acknowledged the situation. It indicates that they were managing the pressure and in control; aware but not overwhelmed by the situation.

When we feel the pressure on the course, we should not see it as a sign that our game is about to go 'off', as frequently happens. On the contrary, feeling the pressure means we are in a position to win. We must see it as an acknowledgement that we are fully aware of the importance of the situation; we must focus our attention on the shot in hand and go through our pre-shot routine. And, in the words of Byron Nelson, 'Don't worry.'

> **Pressure is part of golf and every player experiences it. Don't fight it, or focus on it, rather accept it as natural and implement whatever stress management strategy works best for you: slowing your breathing, a pre-shot routine, positive self-talk or staying in the present.**

7

BEWARE THE ANGRY GOLFER

**'Learn to control your emotions or
they will control you.'**

Edgar Martinez

I am sure you've seen professional golfers hit a bad shot, then smash their club into the ground or throw it against their bag, as their temper explodes in a masterclass of anger. We all know the feeling produced by a simple but complete mis-hit, a once-in-a-lifetime winning opportunity gone – forever.

The injustice, the stupidity, the wastefulness, the agony: all roll into one moment of 'Aaaaarrrrrgggggghhhhh! Why me?' At this point, the language one tends to hear on the course would make many a sailor blush, and of all the expressions of self-disgust I've witnessed, my personal favourite was a fellow who, after chipping into a bunker from an easy uphill lie, simply went very silent and muttered to himself, 'You are nothing more than dog breath,' before following the ball into the bunker like a condemned man who has just heard his last-minute appeal has been turned down.

When we lose our temper, quite simply we are no longer in control of our emotions. For a brief (very brief, one hopes) moment our emotion (anger, rage etc.) is in control of us. I think we can safely conclude this is not the optimal state to be in when playing golf, not to mention driving a car, landing a commercial jet in a crosswind, negotiating a pay increase or any other activity I can imagine.

Whenever I ask a player why they lost their temper, the number-one excuse I get is 'I couldn't help it, it happened before I realised it.' Which is right. The physical response to the emotion of being upset, turning to anger and manifesting itself as an outburst (swearing, club throwing, rage – and let's not forget comparing oneself to dog breath), probably happens in under a second. Tellingly, it is also sometimes referred to as 'emotional hijacking'.

The speed of our response to the incident that made us angry happens so quickly that we have no conscious opportunity to intercept it, shut it down and stop it doing any serious damage to our desired peaceful state of mind. This is why people will say, 'I couldn't help it, it happened before I realised it.'

If we are in a match-play situation and see our opponent play a bad shot and get obviously angry, do we feel sympathy for the plight of our opponent, or do we think this gives us an advantage? (Put more simply, does it 'please' us?) If we are completely honest, we will probably be pleased, as our opponent's display of anger is an indication that things are not going well for them. If, on the other hand, this same player, after hitting a poor shot that costs them the hole, were to show no emotion whatsoever and carry on as normal, we would doubtless think they were in control and far from beaten.

I really don't think anyone plays better 'mad', irrespective of what they may think or believe. Most players get angry at some point during a round, that's natural, but the fact remains that anger serves no positive purpose, other than to demonstrate conclusively that we are upset. Which is exactly the opposite of the calm and relaxed frame of mind that we should be seeking.

Golf is a game of control, which is greatly influenced by our emotions. Given a choice between anger or tranquillity as the best state to play good golf, the majority of golfers would say it is much better to be calm. In fact I can't imagine any player claiming they preferred to play when angry because they played better that way. In certain sports, where physical contact is the object, such as rugby, boxing or American football, 'controlled aggression' may be the optimal state, but this is quite different from anger. The clue is in the word 'controlled'.

I have met golfers who tell me they would like to play aggressively and more or less ignore their opponents, both in match and stroke-play, as they do not want to end up being distracted by their opponents' play. Many years ago, when I was running some courses with ex-soldiers, they too said controlled aggression was the ideal state when going into combat. They said that you had to condition yourself through training and make your training as realistic as possible, so when it came to being 'operational', the memory of the training would allow them to be aggressive but remain fully in control.

There is no one-size-fits-all approach to the mental game, but there are certain mental fundamentals we need to have in place. **Regardless of our personality type, staying calm and in control is the optimal state on the course.** Whether we are someone who likes to play aggressive golf, or we prefer the precise, safe course management approach, the important thing is to stay in control of our emotional state.

Which means **anger has no place in our game.** Not only does getting angry mean we are (momentarily) out of control emotionally, it also means our focus of attention is in the wrong place. Our focus has gone from the next shot to the fact we are upset, and our mind is not on the game but on the upset.

How do we prevent this happening? A good place to start is to be more fully aware of our emotions. When feeling anxious, tense, negative in outlook or angry, we can make a conscious decision to stop letting our frustration spoil our concentration. The key word here is 'conscious': we have to choose to go from a negative state of mind to a positive one, and remind ourselves that we play better when we think and feel optimistic. The sooner we relax and calm down, the more quickly we will be in the best emotional state of mind to play great golf.

MANAGE THE HEAT ▶

Often a poor shot upsets us, or simply makes us angry. This tension-inducing feeling rarely serves us well; we do not play better when angry. This exercise is about enabling you to put a stop to anger.

1 Sit upright in a chair, close your eyes and breathe slowly and deeply. Do this for about two minutes all the while consciously relaxing your body on the exhale.

2 Visualise or imagine yourself facing a simple shot on the golf course, a shot that you are confident you will make. A shot that if faced on the course would create no tension.

3 Now visualise yourself playing the shot poorly. Whichever shot you select, a tee shot, a short putt or a chip to the green, visualise it being played poorly.

4 Make a conscious choice to remain impassive, to not get upset, or angry. Rather see yourself watching the shot with bemusement but not anger or frustration.

5 Repeat Step 4 a number of times, concentrating on the emotional control, not the shot.

6 Before finishing this exercise play the shot perfectly in your mind, dwelling on all the associated positive feelings.

7 Spend a few moments slowly returning to full awareness in the chair.

This is an exercise you should only use when you are experiencing periods of anger and frustration after a bad shot; we are not practising bad shots here! We are creating a positive memory of not losing our cool, and of staying in emotional control.

When we lose our temper, we are no longer in control – of our thinking, our swing or our emotional state. Drop it as soon as possible, and get back to being calm, alert and aware.

8

REMEMBER WHAT HARRY SAID

'To play well you must feel tranquil and at peace. I have never been troubled by nerves in golf because I felt I had nothing to lose and everything to gain.'

Harry Vardon

Pressure in competitive sport is not a modern phenomenon. For as long as human beings have competed against each other, the influence of internal and external pressure has been present. This is especially true in golf, and consequently there is much we can learn from those who mastered pressure in an age before sports psychologists, positive thinking, performance gurus and video analysis.

In professional golf there are players who have risen to the top briefly, before disappearing from sight. One example is the Australian Ian Baker-Finch, a solid player who in 1991 won the Open Championship, finishing with rounds of 64 and 66 to take the title. Rather than launching him into the upper ranks of the tour, the Open success was the pinnacle of his career. Other than finishing runner-up in the 1992 Players Championship in the USA, Baker-Finch never really contended again. His loss of confidence was so dramatic that, irrespective of how well he struck the ball on the practice range, he could not take his ability onto the course. In the 1997 Open, he shot a first round of 92, withdrew from the Championship and retired from tournament golf.

Then there are the truly gifted players who compete year after year and in time become considered greats of the game. Every generation has its legends. Though we often think of the greats of the game as being from the past fifty years, if we look back over a hundred years we find the likes of Tom Morris Jr, Harry Vardon, John Henry Taylor and James Braid, players from an era of tweed jackets, shirt and ties and the occasional pipe, playing with swings which look cumbersome, inefficient and laboured – but all golfers whom we can think of as legends of their time.

Back then, as these players knew, winning was not simply about the swing but about qualities such as character and temperament, and this was particularly true of Harry Vardon. Born in 1870, Vardon was a former caddie and self-taught golfer who went on to win the Open Championship six times (a record that still stands today), and he enjoyed a playing career that spanned thirty years at the very highest level. In 2000, *Golf Digest* magazine ranked him as the thirteenth best golfer of all time.

When we think of golfers such as Vardon, it is tempting to consign them to a romantic but bygone era. Perhaps we suspect that if they were alive today they would find the modern game ill-suited to their abilities. Certainly, swing mechanics have changed immeasurably, club technology has rocketed into the space age and course design had been taken to levels that were unimaginable a hundred years ago. As a result, we might conclude there is little we can learn about the game from these players. But we would be wrong, because one thing all these players had in common, a quality that is as relevant today as it was a century ago, is that crucial and timeless insight: they knew how to win.

Whilst researching this book, I spent a lot of time reading accounts of these players' approaches to the game, but I found very little to indicate what their mental approach might have been. One of the few players to have shared his thoughts on the mental side of the game was Harry Vardon. He made a number of insights about what we would now refer to as the mental game. A number of them seem to me as true today as they were a century ago, and indeed will be a hundred years from now.

You will see in the following thoughts some familiar themes that are still around today. There is nothing controversial here, but when we hear these words from a master of the game we should listen. I have added a few words to put these maxims into context.

'Do not reflect upon the possibilities of defeat; you become too anxious and lose your freedom of style.'
Be positive and focus on winning; otherwise it will be difficult to remain both physically and mentally relaxed.

'Try treating your adversary – with all due respect to him – as a nonentity. Whatever brilliant achievements he may accomplish, go on quietly playing your own game.'
Focus on your own game; do not be distracted by others, or by outside events over which you have no control.

'Perfect confidence and a calm mind are necessary for the success of every stroke.'
Believe in yourself and stay mentally at peace.

'A golfer must never be morbid. If he cannot school himself to think that he is going to make the best drive of his life, he should try not to think of anything at all.'
Avoid negative thinking, and play with a silent mind.

'Remember that more matches are lost through carelessness at the beginning than through any other cause. Always make a point of trying to play the first hole as well as you have ever played a hole in your life.'
Be attentive and focused over every shot, especially on the first tee.

'You must be thoughtful if you want to get on in golf. When you have made a really wonderful good shot – try at once to find out exactly how you did it. Notice your stance, your grip and remember the character of the swing that you made. Usually when a player makes a really bad stroke you see him trying this swing over again – without the ball – wondering what went wrong. It would pay him better to do the good strokes over again in the same way every time he makes them, so as to impress the method of execution firmly upon his mind.'
Create positive muscle memory for the swing by taking a few additional swings after a good shot to embed the 'feeling' and the muscle memory whilst in a positive frame of mind.

'The best golf is that which is played in comparative silence.'
A silent mind, undistracted by any thoughts, plays the best golf.

'The man who is lacking in courage does not often win on the green.'
Confidence is key. You have got to believe you can make the putt.

Harry Vardon places a lot of emphasis on being confident and positive while staying relaxed and playing one's own game. It is interesting to note how much importance he puts on the opening tee shot, but for me the most insightful thing he offers us is the need to reflect on a good shot when we have played it, to discover what it is we did that made the shot possible. How often do we, after playing a bad shot, take two or three further swings as though trying to correct the fault? In fact we are probably further embedding that fault (which we have not correctly analysed) into our muscle memory. Instead, why not, as the saying goes, 'accentuate the positive'?

The challenge now, and always, is to turn knowledge into action. If we don't practise being confident and positive, telling ourselves to be so on the course is unlikely to work. Confidence is a state of mind we must adopt and make a part of our whole thinking process, both on and off the course. Like any endeavour in life, **we improve through repeated practice, so telling ourselves on the first tee to be positive is unlikely to be effective if we do not make a habit of being positive on the practice range, or when talking about our game**. I would wager that the golfers we admire most for their ability to play well under pressure and for being confident and positive are exactly the same off the course as they are on it.

We must therefore practise being calm under pressure. We must be aware of our thought process and, if it is turning negative, switch it off and turn up the positive. If you are someone who treats your first tee shot as something to get over as quickly as possible, you are missing a wonderful opportunity to develop a winning mindset that will pay dividends throughout the entire match.

In this chapter I will leave the final word to Harry Vardon and his thoughts on club selection, which are less about the club than about ourselves and what we believe. If we can change our belief in failure then, in time, our confidence will return.

'If you have completely lost confidence for the time being in any particular club, even though it may be one with which you have performed brilliantly in days gone by, leave it out of your bag for a short period and try to forget about it. The day will come when you will feel that it is once more the very club to make your game perfect.

'Always make up your mind definitely and finally which club to use and then take your stance. If you ponder in a state of uncertainty, your mind will be affected and then your swing and the result thereof will be bad.'

> **Never undervalue the capacity of confidence to disarm pressure; the more confident we are with our swing, our judgement, our equipment and on the course, the less pressure-inducing self-doubt we will experience.**

9

OPEN THE SAFETY VALVE

'You have to block everything out, and be extremely focused, and be relaxed and mellow at the same time.'

Jennifer Capriati

Next time you wash your hands in a regular wash basin, take a moment to notice the small opening which prevents the basin from overfilling and allows excess water to drain away, thus preventing the bowl from overflowing and causing water damage to the floor or building. Most mechanical devices – domestic boilers, hydraulic systems and nuclear reactors – have safety devices to prevent the pressure building to dangerous levels.

Now, think of pressure on the golf course. Do you have a safety valve feature or overflow channel built into your game? We all feel pressure, even those who appear as cool as the proverbial cucumber: they just don't show it, or admit to it.

We all have a personal level of stress we can absorb or manage before we reach capacity, but once we do, we are highly likely to perform well below our potential and, in competition scenarios, 'choke'. For such moments, we need to create a mental approach that we can employ as a valve, so the pressure, though steady and constant, does not overwhelm us or obstruct our playing well.

How do we find such a personal safety valve that we can employ under pressure? It is a question I have been asked by many of my clients. I usually suggest to them that they find a pressure-releasing system, one that feels familiar and right to them, since there is no one-size-fits-all method. I suggest that they look at activities they enjoy for relaxation (other than golf) – it may be cooking, dining out, sailing, photography, travel, seeing friends, repairing old cars, or any one of a multitude of other activities. The chances are, when we begin to think about the thing that we do for relaxation, our brains will recall the emotions associated to that activity. **When we feel the tension begin to build, we can think about something else that has a positive association for us**: a moment from our life, a scene from a film, a favourite piece of music that we find relaxing. **By consciously shifting our thinking from the current stressful situation, we will help relieve the build-up of pressure.**

Many professional players talk to their caddies between shots about seemingly mundane matters, but this allows them to stay in the present and not get ahead of themselves. Likewise, many players have superstitions about colours, ball numbers, tee size, as well as the lucky charms they carry. Distracting themselves through such little rituals contributes to their confidence. However odd, if it works, then use it to beat the pressure.

In golf we have too much time to think. In a round of golf, how much time do we spend actually hitting shots? I mean the time we take from arriving at our ball, through selecting the club, taking our final address (including feet shuffling, waggles and determined glances towards the target), to follow through. I calculate that actual shot-making adds up to between thirty and sixty minutes out of a four-hour round. So we spend between 12.5 per cent and 25 per cent of our time on the course actually engaged in thinking about and playing the shot. If we look simply at the time we spend hitting the shots, this figure probably drops to between five and eight minutes – just 2 to 3 per cent of our time on the course!

Whichever way we break this down, we have a lot of time in a round when we are not actually playing a shot. So what are we doing? *Thinking* – usually about the shot we have just played or the shot we are about to play. This can be good stuff (positive thoughts, or a conversation with a playing companion or caddy about topics other than golf), or bad stuff (negative thoughts, or anticipating a bad outcome on the shot we are about to make).

There is a third possibility, which is simply trying not to think at all, instead observing what is around us and, as Walter Hagen said, 'take time to smell the roses'. By doing this, we change our whole state (mental and physical) from self-awareness and over-thinking to that of 'oneness in the moment'. This can sound somewhat esoteric and mystical, the stuff of monastic training, but it is simple, and the best way to do it, in fact, is to try not to do it. If I asked you to think of nothing, the very act of thinking of nothing would create a series of ideas or images in your mind. However, if I simply remained silent, the chances are you would naturally end up thinking of nothing very much.

On the course, positive thoughts are much better than negative thoughts; I am sure we all have no trouble accepting that. But **if we don't believe our positive thoughts, they will lack the authenticity that comes with confidence; they will simply be words without conviction**. This is a challenge to many players who have tried to employ positive thoughts but find they do not really help – in fact they are a distraction. Believe it or not, all thoughts, both positive and negative, are distractions!

Therefore we need to practise the skill of thinking of nothing at all, and **learn to be in the moment**. If there is one technique above all that I would encourage the serious player to adopt, this is it. Being in the moment is a great way to have our personal pressure valve at 'open' all the time. I tell players simply to **observe without judgement**. That means do not overanalyse the shot in hand, and do not over-think what has happened in the short- and long-term past. **The more we stay in the moment, the less cluttered our thinking becomes**.

I have explained before that the best way to train oneself to do this is through daily relaxation and visualisation exercises, at home or in a quiet place. Trying to think of nothing is tough at first, but over time it becomes easier, and eventually we will find we can do it. By doing this, we are replicating the 'zone', the state of being where there is no thought, simply an awareness of being in full control. I have spoken with professionals who tell me of times they were in the zone, and again and again, they talk about a sense of timelessness, of the experience being non-emotional, and that they possessed a certainty that everything was going to be good. Without exception, this state was something they could not replicate at will, but they knew it when it happened. Similarly, I am not suggesting that we will be able to enter the 'zone' at will, but I do believe we will greatly increase the probability of doing so if we invest time in diligent practices, training our minds off the course.

I'm aware that, in the heat of a high-pressure scenario, simply trying to distract our 'thinking self' feels difficult, and the reason for this is because it is! It is difficult to do anything of which we have no experience, or which we have not consciously practised. There is an old saying: you get out of life what you put into it.

> **If we don't train ourselves to manage the stress, to be calm under pressure and empty our minds over the ball off the course as part of our practice regime, it is unlikely we will ever be able to do it on the course.**

10

YOU TRULY NEED TO BELIEVE

'It doesn't help a great deal to have the soundest swing in the world if that swing is not trusted.'

Bobby Jones

There is a huge difference between saying something and believing it. We are all familiar with sporting managers predicting victory before a match – even when we know from current form that they are going to lose. Or the politician on the eve of an election looking the interviewer straight in the eye and saying, 'We are going to win,' regardless of the fact his party trails in every poll. When we hear people make such statements, not only do *we* not believe them, we suspect *they* don't believe what they are saying themselves. But they are not being delusional – far from it: they are being practical. They are saying what is expected of them, rather than what they truly believe, for the benefit of their supporters.

On the golf course we can see a similar situation. Some people say before a match that they are going to win; others *believe* that they are going to win. In my experience, this simple yet subtle difference is crucial.

Imagine you have a final interview for a job you really want. The new job pays twice as much as you are currently earning, involves international travel, an annual bonus scheme, plus wonderful opportunities for career advancement and a prestige company car. It would be safe to conclude that you really, really want this job. Unfortunately, there is the matter of the nauseating and potentially life-changing final interview to get through.

Let me propose two scenarios for this interview.

Scenario one: you are one of two final candidates. The other person is three years younger, attended an Ivy League university, holds a Harvard MBA, speaks five languages, including Cantonese and Mandarin (which she studied during a six-month immersion course in China), and has represented her nation in the previous Olympic Games and founded her own charity!.

Scenario two: you are told two days before the interview that you are the only candidate going through to final interviews; that in the previous two rounds you were hands down the most impressive candidate; that your prospective employer has decided to offer you the job already and that this interview is a formality that has to be completed as part of the interview process. The person telling you this is close to the source, so you know without any doubt that it is true.

Let's return to scenario one. This dream job is in the balance: it may go to the other candidate, who appears, on paper at least, to be the stronger of the two of you. When you go into the actual interview you will not be fully confident you are going to get the job. This will make you more aware of the need to give a great interview, impress the interviewers and generally win the day. So in the days leading up to the interview you will run through the various interview scenarios in your head, anticipating the questions you may be asked and considering the pros and cons of getting the job. The pressure this creates will build, the closer you get to the actual interview. The uncertainty will likely make you worried, anxious and generally uneasy.

Which is similar to the feelings we can experience before an important match, or the final round of a major when holding the lead for the first time. The anxiety is a natural emotional and physiological response to stress (as that is exactly the source of these feelings). The worst part of all is there really seems to be very little we can do to alleviate these feelings, which makes the interview, or the final round, all the more challenging.

If we look at scenario two, the emotion you are most likely to experience is confidence – the polar opposite of worry or anxiety. You will be feeling self-assured; indeed you might even be looking forward to the interview because, it would appear, the job is a done deal and nothing can possibly go wrong. You know that you have already got the job – you *know* the outcome.

Very few golfers experience this feeling of certainty going onto the golf course. But I believe it is the best possible state of mind to have: the quiet self-assurance that all is going to be well, that the outcome will be positive. It is, in fact, exactly the sentiment Harry Vardon expressed over a hundred years ago when he wrote, '**Do not reflect upon the possibilities of defeat; you become too anxious and lose your freedom of style.**'

Most club players have an opponent they can never seem to beat, no matter how well they play, or someone they know they will always beat, just as most golfers will have a favourite hole on a course or a bogey hole that always seems to feature in a scorecard disaster. These players and holes are examples of scenarios where we have a confident outlook which allows us to feel settled and relaxed, or an insecure outlook which causes us to believe that we are jinxed somehow, and in turn leads us to tighten up, grow anxious and play in the wrong frame of mind.

If being relaxed, positive and truly confident is the best state of mind in which to play our best golf, how do we reach that state? It is the $64,000 question. I believe it comes more easily to some than others, but I do believe everyone can improve their capacity to achieve the mental state necessary for positive confidence. It does, however, require learning and practice, and not simply giving ourselves a well-intentioned pep talk on the way to the first tee.

In 1991, at the age of 33, Ian Woosnam was ranked the number-one golfer in the world. When he arrived at Augusta for the Masters Championship he was not the favourite to win; that honour belonged to Nick Faldo, looking for his third successive title. Woosnam led the tournament by three strokes from José Maria Olazábal and Tom Watson going into the final round, but a three-shot lead means less at Augusta in the final round than just about anywhere else in the world. By the time Woosnam got to the eighteenth hole, his lead was gone, and he was tied with his playing partner Tom Watson, who had made eagles at the thirteenth and fifteenth holes.

Watson drove his ball with a slice and it ended up in the woods on the right with no shot to the green; Woosnam decided to drive over all the hazards, and hit a huge drive which ended up in the rough way over the left-hand side of the fairway. He faced a tough 130-yard shot to the elevated green, which he played well onto the fringe. His first putt ended up six feet right of the hole. Watson meanwhile had missed a putt for bogey and, with Olazábal one shot behind, Woosnam had this six-foot putt for the Masters Championship.

Woosnam duly made the putt and won the title. Afterwards he said, 'I told my friends I was going to show America how I can really play. I realised it was time I believed in myself, I had always thought of myself as second class.'

Here was the world's number-one player admitting that he had felt a lesser person or golfer than others. Yet when he truly believed in himself he discovered the missing part of his ability to win a major.

When we believe genuinely that we are going to win, we are more likely to win; when we believe that we will lose we are usually right again. This simple truth follows the fact that we move in the

direction of our dominant thought, because our dominant thought becomes our expectation. Our subconscious mind holds onto the dominant thought as being 'real' and 'true', and performs in accordance with the expectation it holds. As Tiger Woods succinctly expressed it, 'The biggest thing is to have a mindset and a belief you can win every tournament going in.' When that mindset and belief is no longer present, we have to rediscover it, or we become our own biggest obstacle to winning.

> **Being in a positive and truly confident state of mind is only possible when we are relaxed, and we can only be relaxed when we are at peace and not allowing pressure to manage us.**

11

DON'T FIGHT THE NERVES

**'Anger is a wind which blows out the
lamp of the mind.'**

Robert Green Ingersoll

One of the wonderful functions of our nervous system is to make us fully aware of our environment and keep us safe from danger. Many millions of years ago, hunting food in the forest, our forefathers had to beware of becoming the prey of a woolly mammoth, a sabretooth tiger or a carnivorous dinosaur. A consequence of the evolving nervous system was to create the fight or flight response for such situations, where a choice was quickly made between fighting or running, in order to give the best chance of survival.

What has the fight or flight response to do with golf? And, specifically, what has the evolution of a nervous system to do with playing well under pressure? The nervous system in our body draws attention to threats to our safety and well-being, both real and imagined. When we are on the golf course it is easy to feel threatened by defeat, by an opponent, or by the course itself. Even though this threat is not endangering our life, it is making us feel uncertain and insecure; consequently adrenalin is released into our bloodstream, triggering the fight or flight response.

When we choke in a golf game, I believe we are experiencing the fear response. Not that we feel scared whilst playing golf; instead we are experiencing the emotional response we associate with the discomfort and uncertainty of situations over which we feel we have no control. The natural response is to ignore these feelings, to dismiss them, or simply to try overwhelming them by labelling them a sign of weakness, telling ourselves we need to toughen up, pull ourselves together, and simply get on with it.

However, **being nervous is not a bad thing: it reminds us that we have a challenge ahead of us that requires our full attention**. Many of the best performers in both sport and entertainment confess freely to suffering huge bouts of nerves before big occasions. It is not a sign of weakness or inadequacy; rather it indicates a state of preparedness and awareness. But **there is a difference between being nervous and being fearful. Being nervous aids our focus; being fearful generally impedes performance**. I have found those who are nervous before a performance or an event generally perform better than those who either claim to have no nerves, or are fearful. **Tension is a natural part of any competitive endeavour; we must learn to accept it and not fixate on it.**

When our nerves overwhelm us, we move from anticipatory nerves to a state I refer to as conscious incompetence, a state in which we no longer trust ourselves to perform the task at hand. In this state we unwittingly try to micromanage everything we do and become too self-aware; in the process we lose our sense of instinct or natural ability.

How often under pressure have you felt your putter was like a shovel in your hand? Your swing felt like you were chopping wood (badly) in a lumberjack competition, you stood over a short wedge to the green with no idea of where it was going to land, even though on the practice ground you would hit ten out of ten with ease. This is because your increased self-awareness or mild anxiety has caused you to over-think and overanalyse the shot in hand. When this happens, we question our ability and doubt our technique. Without meaning to do so, we undermine our all-important self-confidence and become the architects of our own self-sabotage.

What can we do to counter this? We can remind ourselves that feeling nervous before a game or a shot is quite natural; it lets us know we're fully aware of the importance of the outcome, but is in no way indicative of how you will play.

The best strategy I have found for overcoming nerves is, rather than fighting them (they have a terrible habit of fighting back and returning more powerfully), **to accept them but not focus on them, to remove any value from them and let them flow over us, in a detached manner, observing them but not enduring them.** This is easier to do when we have a pre-shot routine. Very few weekend golfers employ a pre-shot routine, but it can be beneficial for players at all levels. The pre-shot routine enables us to go into a kind of automatic pilot. Because we have rehearsed the swing sequence and pre-shot actions so many times on the practice ground, once we are on the course we are able do them without thinking, and the more of our routine we can execute without thinking, the more likely we are to remain confident, positive and calm – and not be overwhelmed by nerves.

Over the past fifteen years I have given almost 700 motivational business presentations, to audiences ranging from executive boards in private locations to 7000 cynical sales folk in Las Vegas, from members of royalty to disgruntled employees; I've spoken through a translator to an audience who sat in total silence throughout the presentation of 75 minutes, but then burst into sustained applause when I finished (hopefully for the talk and not for the fact I had finished); I've spoken in almost every conceivable scenario, so it would be fair to say that I have a great deal of experience. Yet I still get nervous before every talk I give. For many years I looked at ways to reduce my nerves before I spoke, but I discovered that on those occasions when I had no nerves the talk was missing something, some energy, a connection to the audience, or perhaps just a sense of authenticity. The talks without nerves were never as good as those talks given when I had the tingle of anticipation – the butterflies in the stomach prior to walking on stage.

So **don't treat any experience of nerves on the course as another hazard to manage, rather be aware of it but try not to become fixated on it**. For example, in a strong wind the impulse is to hit the ball harder, whilst the prevailing wisdom is to hit it softer, so as not to put excessive spin on the ball, or force the swing. Both these options take our attention away from the wind and back to our swing, so when feeling nervous we should bring our attention to the shot in hand and focus on the target, not on our nerves.

Bobby Jones, probably the most successful amateur golfer the sport has ever seen, had a firm opinion on the usefulness of nervousness. He wrote, 'I used to think that if I could suppress a feeling of nervousness when starting out to play a match, I could then play a better and more thoughtful game. I have since come to think that the man who goes placidly on his way is often the easiest fellow to beat, for it is only the high-strung temperament that rises above its own ability to meet a great occasion.' Jones believed that experiencing nervousness got you focused and into the match.

> **Nerves are not a sign of weakness or lack of preparedness, rather a sign we are aware of the challenge ahead. We must focus on the outcome we want, and not the outcome causing the nerves.**

12

A POSITIVE SWING THOUGHT

'What you are thinking, what shape your mind is in, is what makes the biggest difference of all.'

Willie Mays

Do you have a swing thought before you prepare to play a shot? Most teachers agree it is a good habit to form, as it helps us focus on one positive 'to do' and prevents us getting distracted by unhelpful or destructive thoughts before the swing. I am an advocate of using one positive swing thought before beginning the stroke – but not *during* the stroke, as then we are best to leave our mind silent, and allow the swing to flow automatically without mental input beyond the subconscious management of our muscle memory.

Our swing thought must be positive, and never negative. We must not think, 'Don't hit it too hard,' but rather, 'Smooth swing.' The brain locks onto what it imagines, so if the instruction is negative so will the associated mental image be. It is like saying to someone, 'Don't think of a giant yellow elephant': as their brain processes this instruction, it is simultaneously building an image of the thing it has been told to disregard. (Are you thinking of a big yellow elephant right now?)

We are all familiar with the cruel paradox that occurs after we tell ourselves not to hit the ball in the water or out of bounds: we proceed to do exactly that, and then wonder why. This is because we visualise the messages we give ourselves, as an aid to helping us achieve an outcome. **If our dominant thought is negative then we are more likely to achieve a negative outcome. If our dominant thought is positive, we increase the likelihood of success.**

The problem many of us have is that we have unconsciously developed a negative thought pattern when we come to important shots. This may have arisen over many years, from similar situations in which we have failed to execute the shot we desired. Unless we consciously change our thought pattern, we will fall in to the same negative thinking habit again and again.

ACCENTUATE THE POSITIVE ▶

This is an awareness drill. Before you play your next round of golf ,or take in a regular practice session, make a commitment to only use positive language. Even when a shot has gone badly, find a positive turn of phrase before moving on. The words we use influence our thoughts and feelings. Using negative words encourages negative thoughts and feelings, and the opposite is true, too.

This seemingly simple drill will a) not be at all simple to execute, and b) reveal to you how often during practice or play you fall into the bad habit of negativity. We want to play well under pressure and to do that we have to be aware and relaxed at the same time, neither of which are possible when we are upset.

This drill might appear simplistic, but it works. It can help us to stay in the moment and avoid getting negative about our game.

We have already discussed how little time, in a four-hour round of golf, we spend standing over the ball and playing a shot – and how much time between shots we spend thinking. We can conclude that a lot more time is spent thinking than playing. The game of golf is generally agreed to be approximately 80 per cent mental versus 20 per cent physical, so we can see the importance of the 'thinking' side of the game.

Whilst out on the course it is important to stay relaxed and to think positively in general. But when faced with a pressure shot, it is even more important to make sure that our final swing thought before the actual shot itself is a positive one. The positive swing thought should be relevant to the particular shot in question, and should relate to the swing required, whether that be the balance, the tempo, a full follow-through or smooth takeaway: 'Stay balanced throughout,' 'Good smooth tempo,' or 'Finish the swing' would all be fine positive swing thoughts. Rather than trying to manage four swing thoughts at the same time (which is way too much information to process), we need to keep one simple thought in our mind.

A good swing thought is the final reminder to give ourselves prior to playing the shot. I wrote about this at length in my last book, *Silent Mind Golf*: when playing the shot, we want to keep our mind silent and allow our swing to flow naturally and instinctively. Nevertheless, a little note of caution: no matter how positive it may be, giving oneself a swing thought *during* the backswing or at any time during the swing will almost certainly be a distraction to that silent mind.

When we play in a four-ball format, it is quite natural to say positive and helpful things to our partner, especially when the game is getting tough down the stretch and we become aware that our partner is beginning to feel the heat. We say these things to help calm them down and give them positive reinforcement. Yet, ironically, we rarely give this advice to ourselves. But we can, if we choose to: we simply need to be in control of the messages we put into our psyche. Just as taking three deep breaths will slow our heart down and help steady our nerves, so positive swing thoughts will *increase the likelihood* of hitting the desired shot.

Much has been written about the impact of thinking on outcome, and many experiments validate this. I once read an account telling of an American professor of psychology who, after an introductory lecture to first-year students, invited six students on stage and split them into two groups of three. He spoke to each group for a minute separately, then asked both groups if they would help tidy up the large auditorium, as there were a number of items that he wished to see cleared away. It was noticeable that one of the groups was energetic and happy, whilst the other was rather matter-of-fact and lacklustre in their tidying.

When the stage was clear, the professor explained to the other students in the auditorium that he had told the first group they were bright, intelligent and destined to do well in their careers. To the second group he had observed that they appeared to be uninterested and that they really needed to think if psychology was for them. Of course, the students had been picked and divided at random. Having been told they were talented and capable, the first group went about the task with enthusiasm. The second group, in accordance with what they had been told, had responded in a wholly negative manner.

This anecdote illustrates the impact of thoughts on behaviour and outcomes. During a lecture, I once asked an audience made up of people in leadership positions within their organisation the question 'With which person in your lifetime are you going to have the single most significant and meaningful relationship?' A number of answers were volunteered, mothers, spouses and children being the most common initially, but after a very short pause in the answers, someone ventured, 'Ourselves.' This was the answer I was looking for. If we like ourselves and feel good about ourselves, our manner and personalities will reflect this, and conversely the opposite is true.

This is the reason we need to be consciously aware of the messages we give ourselves when under pressure, because positive, kind words are going to be better for us than the negative comments that so often follow a bad shot. When under pressure it is essential that we control the one thing we can – our attitude. Then, before we take a shot, we should remind ourselves: one good swing thought, then stop thinking and play.

> **The swing thought must always be constructive (positive) and come before, and never during, the swing.**

13

FIRST-TEE MINDSET

**'If I don't do what I need to do to win,
I won't win, no matter who is on the
other side of the net.'**

Andre Agassi

Stepping onto the first tee in a competition is generally acknowledged to be the time when our senses are fully alert and the heart is beating a little faster. Even with years of experience on the professional circuit, most pros will admit to having a few butterflies in the stomach on the first tee, as every competition offers a chance to win – or make a fool of oneself. It is not beyond the realms of possibility for the most seasoned professional to hit a hideous shot off the first tee. But the opening tee shot sets the tone for the round: split the fairway and suddenly there is a spring in the step and the confidence levels soar; hit a poor shot and the opposite is true, we start to over-think what went wrong and worry if we are going to have a nightmare on the course that day.

How can we best give ourselves the opportunity of hitting a perfect drive? In golf, as in life, there are no guarantees: you can hit twenty-five perfect drives on the practice range, walk straight to the first tee, and then hit a very poor drive. Equally, we can arrive late at the golf club, change in the car park, arrive at the first tee out of breath and hit a drive that is straight out of our golfing dreams. Yet neither event is as random as it may appear. **The successful drive is a consequence of a good swing, which is aided by maintaining a positive and relaxed state of mind.**

The latecomer who has to change in the car park is, in fact, more likely to be relaxed than the person who has just hit twenty-five perfect drives on the practice ground. They are delighted to have made it on time and are less likely to over-think or tense up on the first tee; already they are beginning to calm down and hit the ball with very little expectation. The keen opponent, meanwhile, is wondering if they can hit a twenty-sixth perfect drive, thinking of nothing else but replicating another good swing on the tee, all the time building up the pressure on themselves to do so.

It is much easier to start as we mean to go on than to make continual adjustments as we play. **When we walk on to the first tee, we should do so with confidence and a positive expectation that we will have a good round and play well.** We have all seen players on the first tee who look very uncertain, making small jokes about how badly they have been playing, and generally exhibiting poor body language. Their mannerisms are congruent with their anxiety: speaking a little quickly, avoiding eye contact, giving a weak handshake. It is obvious that they are not relaxed, and in match play such players are often dead in the water before the game begins.

In no sport is the power of body language more obvious than boxing, where the two adversaries stand in the ring facing each other prior to the fight. As the referee brings them to the centre of the ring to go through final instructions, both boxers get a chance to eyeball each other, in what is known as the stare-down: both boxers look intently into each other's eyes, searching for a sign of weakness in their opponent. Mike Tyson, the former heavyweight champion of the world, said that when he stared into the eyes of an opponent, if the other fighter looked away for even one fraction of a second, he knew they were afraid, and this gave him the confidence that he would win.

I am pleased to say that boxing and golf share little else in common and, other than two sportsmen competing to win, there is no major stare-down on the first tee. However, there are subtle body language signs that we should be aware of. A firm handshake; direct eye contact; upright posture; awareness of surroundings: these are all congruent with being confident. So, we should make sure we are thinking confidently when we arrive on the first tee, and our body language will automatically follow.

Without doubt there are players who try to intimidate their opponent on the tee box. A number of former professionals would ignore or barely nod an acknowledgement to their opponent, or they would shake hands, coldly stare into the eyes of the opponent and say, 'Hi' or 'Play well.' Some argue these people are simply focusing on their own game, as was the case with Ben Hogan; others say this behaviour is intentional intimidation, and designed to give the perpetrator an advantage.

I do not think we need to change who we are when we step on to the first tee. Instead, we need to be the most match-ready version of who we are. If you are naturally a quiet person then that is who you are, but you still need to be match-ready. The same goes for other personality types. I am not a fan of telling people to change their normal state when they go to play, or inform them that it is 'time to put on their game face'; I really don't think it works. What we have to be is fully authentic, our most confident self.

When Rory McIlroy was leading the US Masters in 2011, he changed his preparation for the final round, putting himself in a metaphorical bubble: he didn't talk to too many people or sign autographs on his way into the clubhouse; he was not his usual friendly and chatty self, and rather concentrated on keeping himself free from distractions. Then, in the final round, he was overtaken after hitting a number of poor shots that cost him the title.

In contrast, when, a few months later, he found himself leading the US Open going into the final round, McIlroy treated it like another round of tournament golf: he did not create the bubble or isolate himself from well-wishers and fans. He went on to play one of the best final rounds in the recent history of the US Open, giving a magnificent display of control and composure.

Our body language reflects our mental state. Correspondingly, by changing our physical state, we are able to alter our mental state. I believe when Rory McIlroy at the US Masters changed his routine he changed his mental state. When we go on to the first tee in a match, we should not change our normal routine. However, we should be aware of our physical state: **if feeling nervous, a quick fix and good technique is simply to adopt the body language and movements of a confident person. This is because we associate certain body positions with emotional states.** When a child is scared, it is common that they go into the foetal position, in which they are trying to protect themselves. This is instinctive behaviour that we are born with. Equally when we meet someone we find attractive, we unwittingly display more open body language, in turn trying to make ourselves attractive. In both cases we make these changes involuntarily.

Early in my career, before I had written any books, I was invited by a major consulting firm to give the closing keynote at their national conference. I accepted the invitation, prepared my talk, flew to the venue and checked in to the hotel. The next day I woke up feeling nervous, and when I went to the auditorium I realised what a 1200-seat venue looks like from the stage. At this time I didn't use slides (I didn't know how to) and, as the audience filled the room, I sat down at the side of the lecture theatre, getting more and more anxious about the talk. I suddenly became aware that my legs were tightly crossed, my arms were folded and I was leaning forwards in the chair. I was going into the foetal position. My instinct was to head for the exit, but I knew what was happening, and I forced myself to think, 'How would a super-confident person sit?' A confident person would sit upright, legs apart, with hands together on their lap. I changed my posture accordingly and sat in the position of a confident person: head up, shoulders back. I took a few deep breaths, and immediately the fearfulness subsided dramatically.

> **The first tee is where we need to be alert, aware, and in a state of readiness and confidence. Don't over-think what lies ahead; stay relaxed and positive; stand tall, and treat the opening drive like any other shot.**

14

MEANINGFUL PRACTICE

'I'm not out there sweating for three hours every day just to find out what it feels like to sweat.'

Michael Jordan

The majority of club golfers don't practise with any serious intent at all. They go to the range to loosen up, find a swing that feels good and maybe see how far they can hit their driver. Many simply don't practise at all: a few practice swings on the first tee is as close as they come to practising all year. They then spend much of the round wondering why they are not hitting many good shots.

One of the most frequent dilemmas I discuss with those I coach is how you can replicate course conditions on the practice ground. The practice ground is the place we go to hone our technical abilities and swing, as there is no money involved, no consequences to hitting a poor shot, no titles at stake – no pressure. Sure, there is pain when we hit a few duffs, or awful shots, but we are not feeling any pressure as we line up the next practice ball. I often see people on the practice ground having a good time, getting loose, finding their swing and hitting one shot after another without too much attention to detail, whilst others approach each shot on the range as though it were the most important shot they have ever played, with a grimace on their face to match. I suggest that **practice has to be meaningful, and every shot needs to have an intended outcome.**

When I suggest to some of my students that they treat the final thirty shots on the practice ground as though it were to the eighteenth green in the final round of a major, I do so to encourage them to engage their imagination and their emotions, and not just the physical mechanics of the swing. If they treat these final shots on the range as being vitally important, their level of attention and focus will increase, and the more players can really feel the imagined importance of each shot and then actually strike it as planned, the more likely it is they will do it for real. **If we create the sensation of pressure and nerves on the practice ground, then, at a future time, when we are in competition and have a 'clutch' shot, the feeling over the ball will be familiar**. The reason this is helpful is because we practise dealing with the emotional feeling and physical state we will experience over a real shot. **When on the range, after warming up, I recommend treating every shot with importance and discipline.**

I doubt there are many people playing golf who have the ability to zero in and focus on every shot on the range, especially when they're hitting 300 balls per session. To do this requires immense powers of concentration and commitment. To focus on each and every shot and commit to hitting it as well as possible without being distracted by conversations, events or anything happening around you is challenging. The more we do so, however, the better, because we are rehearsing the intensity and importance that we experience on the course. It is a drill that we should make part of regular practices.

Many professional golfers go to the practice range with their coach and work long and hard on the mechanics of the swing, achieving fantastic change in their performance. I have seen professional golfers on the practice range who were hypnotic to watch: the swing, balance, tempo and quality of strike were majestic. Time and again I have heard people say, 'If only they could take that game onto the course, they would win everything in sight.' I have also witnessed professional golfers hitting the ball so impressively on the practice range that people have gone out and bet on them there and then to win the upcoming tournament. Unsurprisingly these people have lost the wager. So what happened?

Though the professional on the practice ground demonstrates that their swing is excellent and their commitment and dedication is unquestionable, what they have not been able to do is to replicate the feeling of physical and mental pressure that they are going to experience on the course.

This is very difficult to do, and most people I speak to tell me they have tried it but it is just impossible, because **you cannot replicate tournament conditions or pressure conditions on the practice range.** I agree it is difficult to replicate the 'real' pressure, because no matter how much we try, we know it is not for real – just as a commercial airline pilot in a simulator, attempting a night landing in turbulent conditions, knows it is only a simulation. But if you were on their aircraft when such a landing was happening for real, you can bet you would rather they had that simulation experience than not. So too with your practice on the course: you will not be able to replicate the real pressure of the final shot to the last hole in a major, but **the more you can make your practice meaningful and create in your mind and your body the feelings you associate with pressure, the more comfortable your body becomes with that feeling. When you are out on the course in competition and the pressure builds, it will not lead to panic or a breakdown in confidence.**

As young children learning to play the game of golf, how many of us stood with a six-foot putt on the eighteenth green in front of the clubhouse on the summer's evening telling ourselves, 'This to win the Open'? We concentrate with all our might to make that putt. Though, as children, we were too young to have known real pressure, when we hit that 'putt for the Open' we were engaging our imagination and staying relaxed at the same time, creating a simulation in our mind. As adults we don't do this – maybe **we think it childish or unrealistic to engage the use of a 'vivid imagination' as a part of our practice routine. I encourage you to try it, as it will make you more comfortable with pressure and raise your capacity to perform well when the pressure is real.**

Whatever we wish to improve at, we need to practise, and develop the mechanical skills involved. This requires that we go from being passive in our practice to being active: we need to take it seriously and we need to actively engage in trying to hit exactly the shot we want every time we stand over a ball on the range. It does not matter if we are perfecting our bunker play, our long irons, long or short putts: the more we are fully engaged it making it meaningful and 'real', the better we will perform when out on the course.

> **The more meaningful we can make our practice, the more we create in our minds and bodies the thoughts and feelings associated with pressure, the more comfortable we will become with that feeling.**

15

WHEN THE LIGHT TURNS GREEN ... GO

'Success in golf depends less on strength of body than upon strength of mind and character.'

Arnold Palmer

Long before we learn how to drive a car, in fact when we are very young children, we learn one of the simple rules of driving: when you come to a set of traffic lights and the red light is shining, you stop, and when it turns green, you go. We learn this is to allow safe passage of traffic from different directions, and for the rest of our lives, wherever we are in the world, we know a red light means stop or draws our attention to a fault or danger.

When we feel we have been the victim of bad luck on a course or our opponent has been the beneficiary of outrageous good fortune, it is a perfectly normal response to feel aggrieved and angry. Neither of these emotions as mentioned previously are beneficial or helpful: they distract us from our task, directing attention away from making a good swing and playing one shot at a time to feelings of 'that's not fair' and, worst of all, allowing ourselves to feel angry. When these thoughts and feelings arise (and they frequently do), the red warning light is shining brightly in our mind, and it is important to pay attention to it. It is a warning that we are getting emotionally overloaded, and the best thing we can do, as soon as possible, is to stop these negative feelings. We need to get the green light shining again as soon as possible.

When bad luck happens and we feel annoyed and angry, we need to learn to take a deep breath and centre ourselves both physically and emotionally and let it go. We must let go of the frustration, because if we don't it will wear us down, and rarely if ever does it make you play better. Feelings of upset will create tension and anger towards the situation we find ourselves in, which we often transfer to our opponent or ourselves. Any way we look at it, that big red light (or the red mist as it is also known) now shining in our head needs to be turned green, and until it is, we are at a disadvantage. As long as we have negative emotions, we're not going to be in a good space to play our best possible shot.

When we are coming to a clutch shot in a match, the last thing we want to be is angry. Even if we have missed the simplest of shots moments before, we will be well served by regaining control of our emotional state before playing the next shot.

So how do we become masters of defusing tension and anger on the golf course? First, we have to accept that we are responsible for how we react to the negative situations we experience. Therefore we are the best (and only) person to fix things. Just as pilots perform a thorough pre-flight check to make sure all systems are functioning as normal before they push back from the stand, it is a good idea after a setback on the course – lost ball, bad bounce, opponent holing a wedge for a par, three-putting from six feet to lose the hole – to give our emotions a quick check before hitting the next shot. This need not take more than a few seconds.

Before the feelings of anger overtake us, we should remember to take a few deep breaths, even force a smile on our faces, relax our shoulders to stop them tightening up and turn the light from red to green. Equally, if we have just hit a seemingly perfect shot that then took a mathematically impossible bounce and ended up in the deepest rough on the course, we can prevent ourselves from staying mad too long by being aware of our emotional state. Hit a shot that ends up in deep rough at a critical point in the match and of course we'll get mad, but the key is how long it takes to calm down and focus again. Therefore as we walk towards the deep rough there is no point in staying angry at what has just happened; it's over. Our attention should be on getting into the relaxed frame of mind for playing the next shot as well as we can.

EMOTIONAL AWARENESS ▶

This is a simple and very rewarding exercise that I encourage players to perform regularly.

It is all too easy to become engulfed in a cloud of frustration and negativity after a bad shot or two, or if things are not going as well as expected. So, let's subject ourselves to a regular 'emotional state check' throughout the day, wherever we are. Things that are beyond our control and annoy us or make us angry happen all the time. A traffic jam, a slow customer in the checkout line, a missed putt, unexpected rain – the list, I am sure, is endless.

Often it can be the simplest thing that annoys us and our reaction can be completely out of proportion to the actual incident. If we are not aware of it this anger/upset/frustration can very quickly spiral into anger/anxiety/rage, which adds to tension and creates the very pressure we are trying to avoid.

Staying emotionally aware throughout the day, both on and off the course, is a great way to prevent the emotional hijacking that is so destructive to our game. By focusing on the bigger picture and remaining calm during incidents that would normally trigger anger and pressure we can keep our emotional state positive.

This simple daily exercise might feel basic, but it works. It helps us to stay in the moment and to avoid getting down on ourselves.

There is an old tale told of two monks somewhere in Tibet over 1000 years ago. One was an elderly monk, who had spent his entire life living the monastic existence of poverty, obedience and chastity. The other was a pious and devout young fellow who was serving a novitiate to see if life in the monastery was for him; he was keen, enthusiastic and had been in the novitiate robes for a full year. One day the abbot asked the older monk to take the young fellow to another monastery a three-day walk away.

After four hours of walking and talking together, the monks came across a fast-flowing stream, which, though not very deep, was rather wide because the water had risen and the stepping-stones were now submerged. A well-dressed young woman stood looking at the distant bank; she wanted to continue her journey but was unable to, due to the lack of stepping-stones. As part of their religious faith and their vow of chastity the monks were not allowed to talk to or interact with women at all, unless the women were in the presence of their family, so the young monk took no notice of her and promptly stepped into the water and crossed the stream. When he got to the other side, he looked back and saw that the elderly monk had somehow hoisted the young girl onto his back and was slowly and steadily carrying her across the stream. When he reached the other side, the monk gently assisted the girl back to the ground, whereupon she thanked him profusely and continued on her journey.

The young monk looked on aghast: the old monk had not only spoken to a woman, he had touched her as well! The old monk smiled at the young monk and raised his eyebrows momentarily, then, after getting his breath back, continued on the journey. The young monk was outraged by what he had just seen, but couldn't decide whether to report what he had seen to the abbot of the monastery or challenge the old monk himself. He continued to walk, now silent and obviously angry, side by side with the elderly monk. The elderly monk, on the other hand, seemed very relaxed, taking in the scenery and generally appearing very relaxed about life in general and what had just happened at the stream.

After five hours, as they came to a village where they would rest for the night, the young monk was unable to contain his anger and outrage at what he had seen. He said, 'I can't believe you did that; I too have taken vows of poverty, obedience and chastity, and yet I have just witnessed you openly disobey one of our rules by not only talking to an unaccompanied woman but lifting her up and carrying her across the stream.'

The old monk listened patiently and said quietly to the young monk, 'But the difference between you and me is I left her behind some miles ago, and it seems to me you are still carrying her around now.'

The lesson, of course, is that **once an action is past, even if it appears to be unfair or bad, we would do well to let it go, rather than carry it around.** If we are going to try to play our best possible shot, we need to be in the best possible frame of mind. If the red light is glaring in our mind, I suggest we stop to collect our thoughts and feelings, and go through a relaxation sequence, until the light is shining green again.

Getting upset isn't the problem; it is hanging onto it that does the damage.

16

ACCENTUATE THE POSITIVE

'A positive thinker sees the invisible, feels the intangible and achieves the impossible.'

Winston Churchill

Over the past fifteen years I have delivered workshops and masterclasses to a wide variety of audiences around the world. During them I have asked the participants to make a list of the qualities and skills 'they believe' they require for success. After a few minutes I make a list of the first ten answers the audience gives me. Almost without exception 80 per cent of the skills the audience feed back to me that they believe are necessary to be successful in life are attitude-based skills; the attributes that come up time and time again are determination, motivation, commitment, empathy, desire and perseverance. These are skills we adopt; they cannot be taught. They are a state of mind. The remaining 20 per cent are technical: skills we consciously learn or are formally taught. If we take the top fifty golfers in the world, technically there is little to separate their ability to execute wonderful golf shots. However, I believe there is a great deal of difference in the way they prepare mentally and perform under pressure when in the thick of competition.

If we want to summarise these attributes of mental toughness, perception and emotional management, we can use the umbrella term of *attitude*. Our attitude impacts on the way that we think – and not the other way round. The sequence is simple: **our attitude impacts on the way we think; the way we think impacts on the way we behave; the way we behave impacts on the way we perform; and the way we perform impacts on the results we produce.**

When we have a negative attitude, we will have a negative thought process and interpret what we see and experience in that context. It is a small step from thinking negatively to behaving negatively: we have all encountered people who show this to be true, in business, in life and on the golf course too. When something goes wrong, such people act as though they are the victims of a huge injustice. They blame circumstances or simply bad luck for their misfortune. In an unintentionally dramatic manner, they might swear, or punish the club by bashing it into the ground or throwing it casually towards the golf bag. They give little thought to the impact of their actions on their playing companions. Looking at our sequence, such players have started the cascade of thinking and behaving negatively, so chances are they will now perform negatively, which will only further annoy them and feed into the negative thought process.

So, what type of 'thinker' on the course are you? I imagine the majority of players will automatically go with positive. But are you really? We tend (naturally) to overlook our own faults: people placing adverts in the personal columns routinely describe themselves as attractive; humourless individuals will tell you with no sense of irony that they have got a very good sense of humour. As golfers, are we honest about our own faults? The person we should ask is our regular playing partner. There is a great deal of value in asking a good friend for honest feedback about the attitude you bring to the course. To put it another way, do your playing partners brighten up when you arrive on the first tee, or when you leave the eighteenth green?

If friends are honest and say you're not on the positive side of neutral, then take it on board and make a conscious effort to think and act more positively. This may sound overly simple, but remember that **golf is very heavily influenced by our mental state, so a positive attitude is critical**.

No matter how brilliantly we swing a club, no matter how perfectly we strike the ball in the course of a round, we will sometimes have bad outcomes to good strokes. That's life. But golf, like life, is not about what happens to us; it is about how we respond. I am not suggesting that having a positive attitude will turn you into a major winner overnight, but I would be surprised if it didn't improve the quality of your golf, your enjoyment of the game and your mental management on the course.

When I was in my late twenties, I was diagnosed with cancer and was in hospital on and off for a few months. A few months after my treatment had finished I was invited on a television show to talk about my experience. The interviewer, whom I had never met before sitting down in the studio, began his introduction by saying, 'I am delighted to introduce a man who beat cancer through the power of his mind.' This attention-grabbing statement annoyed me, for a number of reasons, but mainly because it was something I had never claimed.

After the introduction, the first thing I said was, 'I need to straighten out an error in your introduction. My cancer was cured by the excellent treatment and support I received from the doctors and staff at the Royal Marsden Hospital.' The interviewer looked very perplexed, because obviously the researcher who had briefed him had given him the wrong information. I then explained that whilst in the hospital I had met a number of patients with very positive attitudes who sadly had not survived, and one or two rather gloomy patients who always seemed to think they were going to die, yet who had recovered. What I stressed, however, was that those with the positive attitudes had a much better journey through the treatment and interaction with other patients and staff, while those with a negative disposition always discussed a gloomy outcome.

I had chosen a positive attitude through my treatment. This is not to suggest I was happy all the time, but I did choose to look for the positive each day and in every situation. When I had treatments that were uncomfortable, I reminded myself it was better than no treatment. When I thought about the fact I was in my late twenties with cancer, I told myself I was lucky that I was young and fit to undergo the treatment that was to follow. I think seeing the positive helped me deal with the situation I faced, and my experiences helped me realise that most of the stuff in our lives, that we sometimes treat as life or death, is in fact just stuff.

A six-foot putt to win the Open Championship is not life or death; it's a six-foot putt. Obviously it will change the life of the person who sinks it; it is a career-defining moment and to miss it will be painful and upsetting. Nevertheless, how we interpret and handle such experiences will be the measure of how we grow and mature as players. Be it a six-foot putt for the Open or the same putt for the best round of our life, whether we make it or miss it, life will go on. Our ability to treat both those outcomes the same is the stuff of which true champions are made.

> **Our attitude, though we may not be aware of it, is entirely within our control. We must be careful which attitude we adopt both on and off the course.**

17

FORGIVE (AND FORGET)
THE BAD SHOT

'Forgive or relive!'

Unknown

Have you ever hit a truly awful shot at a critical point in a game? I'm not talking about a little push or pull, I'm talking about a world-class shank, a stub into the ground that sends shock waves halfway round the world, a spectacularly thinned wedge that flies a hundred yards over the green, a miss of truly epic proportions. I'll stop there, but I'm sure you have no problem recalling your own particular nightmare, because such shots are so deeply embedded in our emotional memory due to the pain associated with them at the time.

When I ask a golfer, be it a touring pro or an amateur club player, 'If there was any one shot you could take again, what would it be?', the shot they recall is rarely the worst shot they ever hit. Rather it is the most painful: the one that cost them victory. The pain of the shot in question has burnt such a deep impression in the emotional centres that when they think of it, the associated emotions, ranging from distress and frustration to embarrassment, begin all over again. For some unfortunate players, it is as though the memory of the shot cannot be shaken off; it haunts them when they find themselves in a similar situation in the future.

The more we think about the bad shot and replay it in our mind, the more likely we are to produce it on the course. This is because we are embedding in our subconscious mind the fear of it happening again. When we are faced with an analogous situation, the subconscious mind searches for a similar scenario to refer to, and guess what memory it finds? The one we have been replaying over and over in our mind.

In a tight singles match at the end of a three-day team competition, I once came down the seventeenth fairway all-square in the final match of the day. My opponent hit his second shot from the fairway into a greenside bunker, and I followed him. This fellow was obviously tense and, being further back in the bunker, had to play first. My ball had come to rest near the face but it was not an especially difficult shot. My opponent sent his ball into the face and ran back into the bunker; he then did this five more times before finally getting his ball onto the green. I could see he had given up and had gone from tension to panic to submission.

It was a surreal situation, in a very tight match, to have my opponent take six shots to get out of a bunker. He stood somewhat shell-shocked, knowing he had just handed me the hole on a plate. I could easily have walked into the bunker and putted out the back of the bunker, but I felt at the time that wouldn't have been sporting. I also could have chipped out sideways, but, again, I thought that wouldn't have been in the spirit of going for it. So I took my sand wedge, and proceeded to take seven shots to get out of the bunker myself.

Now, my first wedge was thinned into the face and simply rolled back down into the hole I had just made. Rather than go to Plan B, and putt or play any backwards shot (a three-wood would have done the trick), I panicked. I had a primal urge to smash the ball out of the bunker. I just tried to hit the ball harder and harder in the hope it was going to come out, with a feeling of gloom gradually descending upon me.

My opponent won the hole. (I have to give him credit for not fainting from the shock, or whooping in delight.) Neither of us could believe that he was now one up, but he quickly accepted the situation and teed off at the eighteenth. If I had known then what I know now I would have slowed everything down to regain my composure, put everything in perspective, and played for a halved match, but I didn't. I was in shock. I couldn't believe what had just happened to me, and played the final hole in a daze. I lost the match, naturally, and our team lost the whole competition. The only consolation was that the team competition had not depended on the outcome of our game.

For the only time in my life I was genuinely speechless. When I tried to explain what had happened, I could feel an immense sadness descend on me that I'd let the team down and I let myself down. With victory at hand I had managed to snatch defeat. I sat in the changing room for thirty minutes, my team-mates bringing a beer through to me but realising it was best to leave me alone.

Years later I could still remember every detail of that hole and that bunker, and every time I remembered it I reinforced it. As a consequence of this, bunker play became my nemesis; I had lost my confidence in the bunker, and replaying the drama of the earlier match did nothing but erode it further.

Eventually, I made a conscious decision to stop dwelling on this past failure, to stop feeling bad for the series of dumb judgements I had made and terrible swings I had delivered. Don't get me wrong, this was not a case of needing to exorcise some personal guilt through a truth and reconciliation session, it was simply a resolution to put painful memories to bed, letting go of the memory, and remembering instead the positive bunker shots I had played in the past (and planned to play in the future). Sometimes, we have to accept that we are not quite as good as we like to imagine we are. Yet we are all capable of being good, and being better than we are, if we are willing to put in meaningful practice and learn to manage our expectations.

This ability to move on can be observed in some professionals, who, when asked by an interviewer about a bad shot they played, dismiss the question, or even say they don't remember. They refuse to dwell on a mistake or allow negative memories to become dominant thoughts. The moment is well and truly gone for them, they are not going to carry it around and replay it over and over again, because they know if they do so it will be an act of self-sabotage that will come back and bite them in the future.

> **Avoid reliving bad shots, or being burdened by painful memories of failure. Let them go, and focus on performing well, by recalling positive memories of success.**

18

THE DREADED
FOUR-FOOT PUTT

**'I don't have any big secret about
putting … Just hit at it. It's either
going to miss or go in.'**

Ben Crenshaw

Ben Crenshaw was considered one of the best putters of all time. Curiously, when asked about technique he said, 'I don't think precise mechanical thoughts, I just stay loose, comfortable and easy.' He didn't believe there was a right or wrong way to putt, no right or wrong way to stand or set up even, but he did believe in making a consistent stroke.

Putting is often seen as a game within a game. Personally, though I believe technique is important in golf, when it comes to putting I believe it is less to do with formal technique and more to do with confidence. The putting green is a very democratic place: it favours no one and is a great leveller, a place where all golfers are truly equal and the best player is not always favourite. It is also where the first cracks in a player's game tend to appear. Many legends of the game confess that the short putts they previously smacked into the back of the hole have become harder and harder. The pressure of making such putts finally takes its toll and the fine muscle control required gradually falls away. In some cases, it disappears altogether and is replaced by the involuntary muscle twitch known as the dreaded 'yip'. The four-foot putt that we regularly face in a round can, over time, reduce even the finest of players to a second-guessing, superstitious, equipment-changing wreck. Why?

I think the majority of golfers would agree that a four-foot putt is much easier than a three-wood from the light rough, or a long bunker shot, a drive hit with perfect draw, or just about any other shot you will find on the course. And it is exactly because it is such a simple shot that the thought of missing it can be so painful and, for some players, become their (negative) dominant thought. Sure, it's only four feet and on the practice green they will make it time and again. But out on the course, when it counts for real, it's a different matter altogether: they know if they miss it they will have dropped an easy shot.

We play our best when we are unencumbered by negative thoughts, relaxed, and in the moment; equally we play our worst when we are full of negative thoughts, tense and worrying about the next shot. This is as true on the green as it is on the tee box, yet we don't seem to agonise over a tee shot as we do a four-foot putt. So let me give you the advice that I have found most helpful: *You have got to putt like it just doesn't matter.*

This may seem counter-intuitive, especially as we recognise that every shot is important. When we think back to the practice green, there is no pressure or penalty for a missed putt, and because we are much more relaxed we are more likely to make those shots. If we can take that same attitude onto the golf course, then we will remove much of the pressure that can cause the nervous stroke-making we so wish to avoid. The more we can develop a putting stroke we are comfortable with, the easier it is for us to let go of trying, be confident and simply rely on the stroke itself. Obviously, this is easier said than done! The more short putts we sink, the more our confidence grows and the more we expect to sink them in the future. The opposite is also true: missed short putts lead to a lack of confidence and an expectation of missing in the future. Simply put, our confidence on the green is more important than our technique, as long as the stroke we adopt and use works for us and can be repeated.

Amongst students of the game, one player stood head and shoulders above all others when it came to putting, and that was the South African Bobby Locke. He was by all accounts an extraordinarily gifted putter with one of the most unorthodox styles seen in the game, which went against all the conventional theories of what constitutes a good putting stroke. The fact that no one has ever attempted to copy his putting style would indicate that it was very individual to him. When he putted, Locke kept his feet close together and kept the ball in line with his left foot. On the backstroke he would take the club inside the line of the putt, and as he came through the ball he would appear to hood the face of the putter and have a very short follow-through, almost as though he was stabbing at the ball. He did not overanalyse his technique, but let the results speak for themselves: it was Locke who coined the phrase, 'You drive for show and you putt for dough.' He was not particularly long off the tee, but placed great emphasis on being accurate. And when he arrived at the green in regulation he was a match for anybody, as his three Open Championship wins demonstrate.

In my experience, over the course of a year, more than half of my golfing friends and clients will change their grip, stance, pre-shot routine – or a combination of all three. Many will invest in the latest putting technology. Every golfer is looking for that magic bullet. Doubtless the best approach is investing time to build the confidence on the greens, but sometimes making a change is all that is required to get the confidence previously lacking.

I have twice played with golfers who had wooden-shafted putters they told me they had inherited from family members many years earlier. One had a severely warped shaft with no grip at all; it had a mallet head and truly belonged in a museum. The other putter was also wooden-shafted and had a flat thin blade that was at least sixty years old. Yet at their club they were both noted as being exceptional putters. I was thrilled to see them with two very different styles of play, but with one significant similarity: they both holed a lot of putts.

The other quality these players possessed was that they did not linger over the ball once they had read the line of the putt. Both stepped up, looked down the line once or twice and then stroked the ball. If they made the putt, that was fine; if not, neither lost their cool, they simply continued. It was watching these two players that led me to conclude that the best way to approach putting is simply to putt like it just doesn't matter. We know that every stroke we take on the golf course *does* matter, but, equally, **the more we worry about bad outcomes, the tighter we become and the greater the likelihood that we will hit an imperfect shot.**

We have all experienced days on the course when our putter is red-hot, when even the putts that do not go in shave the hole and come to rest inches from the cup. Even on the long putts, we can see the exact line we need to take and somehow without even trying we stroke the ball on line and with perfect weight. Those days are all too few, but the fact that we can do it once means we can do it again. If we remember back to those days, we will probably notice that we were feeling relaxed and confident: on such days, a four-foot putt feels like a routine tap-in. It is truly a wonderful and exhilarating feeling to walk up to a putt with the full expectation we are going to make it or put it very close. Yet when we putt badly, we find we have adopted the opposite mindset.

Fear has no place on the golf course. Nerves, and even a little tension, can be helpful. But to be fearful that we are probably going to miss serves no purpose at all.

> **When we step up to a short putt, we need to do so with the confident expectation that we are going to make the putt, and free ourselves to putt in a state of relaxed control.**

19

TRAIN HARD, PLAY EASY

**'I hated every minute of training, but I said,
"Don't quit. Suffer now and live the rest of
your life as a champion."'**

Muhammad Ali

Proper practice, with purpose and commitment, is an investment that will pay dividends over time. Yet it is seen by the majority as a chore, and is used to iron out a few kinks before they play. We need to practise to improve our ability, irrespective of how long we have been playing the game and the level at which we play. **The more we can groove our swing into our muscle memory, the less we need to think about our swing on the course, and especially when under pressure, which builds our trust and confidence.**

I believe there is no specific amount of time one needs to spend on the practice ground for it to feel worthwhile; rather it is the quality of the time that is more important. Many players practise badly, without focus and with little concentration. **Whatever we practise we repeat; whatever habits we learn we manifest.** This may explain why the best golfers take practice very seriously. Do you?

I have spoken with a number of young professional golfers who have expressed a desire to improve their mental approach to the game. Frequently they will tell me they have read the books and understand what they need to do, but find it difficult to put theory into practice.

Some, I imagine, hope for a quick fix: a simple mantra they can repeat before each shot which will put them in the perfect frame of mind to make the shot.

It is paradoxical that many people understand the need to spend one or two hours per day on the putting green, practising to create a routine and swing sequence to improve their success rate, yet think the idea of doing mental exercises to strengthen their powers of focus is not only a waste of time (because they understand it) but also impossible to recreate on the course.

The practice area is exactly that, a place to practice and experiment with new techniques or equipment. It is not called the 'hitting' area or the 'ball beating' area or the 'look how hard I can hit it' area. Yet this is exactly what a lot of amateur players do. We need to treat our practice sessions like a trip to the gym, setting ourselves clear goals for each session and having a plan before we go.

Just as a teacher in school has a lesson plan for each class, **we need a practice plan to follow when we get on the range, which includes mental preparation.** Before a theatre production is put in front of an audience, it is learnt, choreographed and rehearsed until all the glitches are removed. Imagine if the actors simply read the play, memorised their lines and then turned up on opening night: what would happen? It would be a mess, because without the rehearsals, the performers' timing and movement would be out of sync. **When we are on the golf course we are performing; when we are on the range we are rehearsing for that performance – so it is important that we make our rehearsals real and meaningful.**

Confidence comes from faith in our ability to execute the shot at hand. Repeated practice builds up positive memories we can refer to in the future, which will increase our expectation of playing well, and in turn build up our self-belief. Without faith in our ability, we replace confidence with hope. We are all familiar with the old 'hit and hope' school of golf, which most of us have played, in which we're never sure how far or where exactly the ball is going to go, but always hoping it will go in the general direction of the green. We all deserve better than that. **If we truly want to play better golf, compete successfully and win more often, then** *we have to practise with purpose*. The more we practise, diligently taking each shot as though it were in actual play, engaging our imagination before the shot and closing our minds down through the shot, the easier we will find it to do on the course in the heat of battle.

I once worked with a golfer who commented that he practised a great deal but wasn't seeing much change in his golf, and wondered if I had any advice. I asked him what his bad shot under pressure was, and the fellow told me he had a habit of slicing or blocking the ball right. I told him to go into the pro shop and buy two dozen of the most expensive golf balls in the shop, then go to the farthest right-hand area of the practice range, closest to the thick rough, bushes and general swampland running down the right-hand side. I told him to try to land each ball ten yards inside the practice area, parallel to the boundary line. If he sliced one, it would be lost forever.

The golfer pondered my suggestion, then told me he wasn't going to lose brand-new golf balls, and would do the same exercise but with range balls. But I explained that the exercise wouldn't work, because if he lost a range ball, it wouldn't matter – there was no sense of replicating the pressure that was resulting in the blocked drive.

The more we can replicate pressure on the practice ground, the better equipped we will be to deal with it on the course for real, because it will not be an unfamiliar sensation. So when we go to the practice area in future, we should consider hitting fewer balls but spending more time in our pre-shot routine, and allow our imaginations to create a scenario of pressure that we are likely to experience in real competition. When we do this we can feel the emotions, the butterflies in the stomach, the tightness in the swing, even the shortening of breath. We can then consciously relax, by taking deep breaths, moving more slowly and taking one or two extra tension-relieving waggles before the swing.

Time on the practice area is all about quality, not quantity; not the time we spend but the intensity we put into what we do. We can go to a gym and spend an hour sat on an exercise bicycle watching TV or listening to music, and tell everyone we have done so, but unless our training is focused we will not get any fitter. But if we go to a spinning class, increase the resistance on the pedals and recreate what it really feels like to climb hills for twenty minutes, then we will end up exhausted and sweaty – but confident that in the future when we reach the hill we will leave behind the fellow who had trained by watching TV while he pedalled well within his comfort zone.

Train hard; play easy!

20

I CAN

'If you aren't playing well, the game isn't as much fun. When that happens, I tell myself just to go out and play the game as I did when I was a kid.'

Tom Watson

'I can.' Two very simple words which, if we use them and believe them when we say them, will help build our self-esteem, and encourage a positive frame of mind.

It is estimated that for the first four years of our lives we mainly receive messages of positive reinforcement, with our parents telling us we are clever, pretty, smart, capable, brilliant and all-round little geniuses – even when the evidence suggests otherwise. We fall over, speak grammatically incorrect language, put our trousers on back to front and perhaps even eat food from the dog's bowl, but in the ever-loving eyes of our parents we are little wonders, and are told as much in a process of repeated encouragement.

From the age of four to sixteen, however, it is believed that 90 per cent of the messages we receive are negative: 'Don't do that,' 'Be careful,' 'You'll have an accident,' 'Are you stupid?,' 'Are you clumsy?,' 'Why can't you be like your sister?' All the time our internal voice, which until the age of four led us to believe we could do anything we wished (statistics suggest that 96 per cent of four-year-olds have very high self-esteem and levels of confidence), is having to adapt to a new way of thinking about ourselves, with the result that we become rather insecure teenagers, full of self-doubt and negative self-image, and in some cases develop lifelong low self-esteem and insecurity issues.

In the world of personal development and self-improvement, there is an expression which runs, 'The you you see is the you you'll be.' It became a popular mantra thirty years ago, suggesting that our self-image has a great impact on our self-worth and consequent life achievements.

It is important that we believe we can win, that we believe we can improve, and that we can handle pressure when it appears. Standing on the eighteenth fairway with a four-iron in your hand is not a good time to experience self-doubt, and begin hearing negative self-talk. I believe that when a person receives a great deal of negative reinforcement through adolescence and early adulthood, even if this is well-intentioned and done to inform and instruct, from a teacher, relative or parent, the negative messages remain within the psyche and the person replaces the voices of those people who are now out of their lives with their own, and consequently continues to give themselves negative self-talk.

I have been with players when a bad shot has provoked some colourful language, where the player refers to themselves in wholly negative terms, most commonly 'you idiot', but also such popular descriptions as 'clown', 'knucklehead', 'bozo', 'chump', 'stupid' and the ever popular – and this needs to be spoken loudly and assertively: 'Oh [*insert your name here*]!' When I ask them would they allow a teacher or adult to speak to their children in such a way, they always say no. Such language is inappropriate, negative and damaging. Yet, this is the message they're giving themselves on the golf course, playing a game at which they are trying to improve. One doesn't need to be a psychologist to figure out how destructive this internal dialogue is.

When I was a young boy, if I ever spoke negatively about someone, my mother would say to me, 'Robin, if you can't say anything nice about someone, don't say anything at all.' Your parents probably said it to you too. Our internal dialogue needs to be positive; bad shots need to be accepted and 'let go'. We will hit bad shots even if we practise ten hours a day, eat well, go weight training, meditate for four hours and read everything about golf theory. Why? Because we're human, and though we strive for perfection, it's an aspiration that is ever so slightly beyond our grasp. Even the most refined metals will, when examined in a gas spectrograph, reveal imperfection. As golfers, when we face a challenging but not impossible shot, we need to remind ourselves that we can make it and truly believe we can.

When we find self-doubt creeping in to our thoughts, we need to stop it, drop the thoughts and remind ourselves that we can make the shot: we can sink the putt, we can get out of the bunker, and yes we can clear the lake with our three-wood and hold the green. **As long as we believe, we keep alive the opportunity to play our best shot; when we believe we can't, it is likely we'll be right.**

There is a poem that appeared in the 1960s, which Arnold Palmer kept inside his locker. It has had been attributed to numerous authors, and its true origins are unknown. You may be familiar with it and, if read with a cynical eye, it can easily appear a little hokey. When it's read with an open mind, its truth and wisdom are obvious.

THE VICTOR

If you think you are beaten, you are.
If you think you dare not, you don't.
If you like to win but think you can't,
It's almost a cinch you won't.

If you think you'll lose, you're lost.
For out in the world we find
Success begins with a fellow's will.
It's all in the state of mind.

Life's battles don't always go
To the stronger or faster man.
But sooner or later, the man who wins
Is the man who thinks he can.

Self-doubt is a destructive force. It slowly but surely robs us of our confidence, and before we know it we find ourselves saying, 'I can't,' rather than 'I can,' unwilling to take any risk in an attempt to avoid failure or a negative experience. **One thing we can always do is our best, and win, lose or draw, take the positive experience of at least giving ourselves the opportunity by trying.** Our regrets in life are not for the things at which we failed, but for the things we wish we had attempted but never tried.

> **If we don't believe we can win, or**
> **manage pressure when it arises, then**
> **it is an odds-on certainty that we won't.**

21

SLOW DOWN

'For fast-acting relief, try slowing down.'

Lily Tomlin

When I was a boy, I came across a song by Simon & Garfunkel called 'Feelin' Groovy'. As soon as I heard the song, I played it again and again; it became my favourite song. It just made me feel good; it calmed me down if I was going through a little patch of teenage angst – and I still love it now. Though it is a wonderful melody, I was most enthralled by the sentiment of the lyric – in particular the first line, only six words long:

'Slow down, you move too fast.'

When tension builds we speed up: we breathe a little faster, talk a little faster, move and swing a little faster. **What we need to do when tension builds is slow down**. Most of us have been aware during a game of losing our feel and tempo, and no matter how hard we try to slow down, we seem to hit the ball harder than usual and we end up hitting a poor shot.

If we accept the probability that as a consequence of being nervous or experiencing tension we are likely to speed up, from our heartbeat through to our swing, then **consciously slowing ourselves down allows us to stay more in control when pressure builds**. It is well known that the act of taking deep breaths in and out slows the heart's pumping and counteracts the effects of adrenalin; equally, walking slowly and deliberately between shots adds to this process.

In the professional game, players know the importance of slowing themselves down when under pressure, especially after a poor shot. If a player fails to get the ball out of the bunker on their first attempt they do not step up and take an immediate thrash at it. They step away from the ball, reassess the shot and go through their pre-shot routine slowly and deliberately. If it's good enough for them, I think there's a lesson there for us all to learn.

When we get nervous, the adrenalin in our bloodstream increases our heart rate. A consequence of this is to speed up most of our processes, both mental and physical. If we give a speech, and feel nervous, we start to speak more quickly than in everyday conversation. If we are running late for a meeting, we walk quicker or drive faster than normal. If we attend an interview for a job and are asked a difficult question, we might start to answer without fully forming the response in our head, and keep talking until we hopefully find it.

When people ask me for advice before giving a public speech, I tell them to print at the top of the notes in big letters 'BREATHE and SPEAK SLOWLY'. When we are nervous, our breathing becomes shallower and we speak more quickly. We want to get through the presentation and sit down once again, because speaking in front of a group of strangers or colleagues is, for many people, a terrifying experience. When I first began speaking at large corporate events, I printed at the top of each page of my notes the very same instructions – 'BREATHE and SPEAK SLOWLY.' The other word I added was 'SMILE'. People find it incredible that I reminded myself of such simple instructions at the head of every page, but I did.

I did so because I knew from experience that when we are very nervous it is easy to get what I call 'brain lock', when we become unable to think straight and almost freeze, as though caught in the headlights of an oncoming express train. Having these words printed at the top of each page gave me a clear, simple instruction to follow if this happened when I was on the platform. I am pleased to say that I never experienced 'brain lock', but I frequently read those words when I was presenting to keep me grounded.

We need to create a way of keeping ourselves grounded when the heat is on. Nowhere is this more important than on the golf course, in the heat of battle coming down the stretch, when the adrenalin begins to surge, and we involuntarily start to walk a little faster, grip the club a little tighter and swing shorter and faster than we normally would.

As I mentioned previously, the root cause of choking is the fear that something bad is going to happen, and **fear is the greatest cause of destroying a player's concentration, confidence and swing**. If the fear is not checked or disabled, then it will take hold. Most people know their favourite song, scene from a movie or comedian, as these are positive emotional memories. We all have recollections that make us smile, so when stress builds and the fear of failure appears on the horizon, any strategy we can employ to recall positive happy thoughts and memories will take our mind and emotions away from a negative fearful state to an optimistic positive one.

In golf, as in other sports, there are players who have not prepared themselves in terms of what to do when the nerves start interfering with the performance process, and how to manage the pressure that comes when they find themselves in the lead in the back nine in the final round. A history of winning is always going to be a huge help, even if only at the junior level, as a memory of winning will be easy to recall, and these memories will restore feelings of confidence. But if no memories of winning exist, create them! **The ability to visualise winning on a regular basis gives our subconscious mind the experience of winning, so when we find ourselves in a position to win, our mind has positive experiential memories already stored.**

This was true of Seve Ballesteros who, in 1980, in preparation for his fourth appearance at the Masters Championship, worked with a doctor who created subliminal visualisation tapes of Seve winning the Masters that same year. Ballesteros listened to the tape every night as he went to sleep, and it continued playing whilst he was asleep. He visualised every aspect of the tournament, from arriving at the clubhouse, the sights and sounds of the tournament, the roars of the crowd, the sinking of putts, the prize-giving in the Butler Cabin and receiving his green jacket.

By the time he came to the back nine on the final round of the tournament, Ballesteros was ten shots clear of the field, and went on to win his first Masters. A similar thing happened to Lee Trevino during his first appearance at the Open in 1970: he told anyone who would listen that he was going to win the Championship, and when on the final day he saw his name at the top of the leader board, he said he felt comfortable because he had been saying it so long that he believed it himself.

> **When we feel comfortable, we are more likely to be calm and relaxed, and take things at a comfortable pace. When we are stressed, the opposite is true: we rush, and the more we rush the less attention we pay to detail. Simply slowing ourselves down is a very quick method of regaining control; combined with some deep breathing, the effects can be instant.**

22

DON'T GET MAD ... JUST RELAX ... STAY CALM

**'Don't let the bad shots get to you.
Don't let yourself become angry. The true
scramblers are thick-skinned, and they
always beat the whiners.'**

Paul Runyan

Have you ever met someone who asked you, 'Do you know what makes me really mad?', then went on to give you a shopping list of things that annoy them: airline food, bad service, queuing in supermarkets, bureaucracy, rudeness, the cost of living, and many other frustrating but ultimately insignificant irritants from daily life?

It is impossible to go through life completely indifferent to what's happening around us, allowing nothing to make us mad or at least a little upset. However, most of the things we think make us really mad are of no consequence at all: nothing can make us mad, unless we allow it. Eleanor Roosevelt, the wife of the former US President, famously said, 'No one can make you feel inferior without your consent.' In other words, we determine our response to others. It never feels this way, because we react to the situation so immediately that it feels beyond our control – but it isn't.

If someone were, accidentally, to stick a needle into your arm, you would naturally get a shock, feel pain and yell out in distress. If, on the other hand, a nurse or doctor had to give you an injection in the arm, and prepared you in advance, you probably would not. The reason is that you are prepared. When something happens for which we are not prepared, we respond accordingly. This extreme example mirrors the anger reflex: we get angry when something upsetting or unpleasant takes us by surprise. Anger feels like the appropriate emotional response. And on the golf course, there are many things that can make us feel this way.

It is not only things on the golf course that make us mad: the dreaded shank, a hook, a lost ball, staying in the bunker, and many other scenarios can make us want to scream in frustration. There is another aspect of the game that is equally likely to connect to our sense of frustration if we are not careful – and that is other people. Sometimes when we are in competition, our opponent may have an irritating mannerism or a characteristic that just bugs us, which, curiously, wouldn't if they were our playing partner. It may be as simple as our sensing their overwhelming desire to beat us, which they have every right to if they are true competitors, just as we want to beat them. **Without the desire to win we will lack focus or direction, but we should not focus on getting 'mad' with our opponent, or with our bad shot or missed tap in. We you should focus our attention on staying in the moment and being in the best state of mind to play our next shot.**

Some people claim that getting mad helps them to compete at a higher level, because it makes them concentrate more and fires up their desire to win, but in truth they have learnt to channel their anger into something helpful, such as concentration. Others tend to become focused on the fact that they are mad, are unwilling to accept responsibility for it and look for things to blame outside of themselves. **Blaming outside factors is a waste of time and energy that would be better invested in returning as quickly as possible to a calm and**

emotionally relaxed state. When we get angry, our focus has gone from winning, or making a good balanced swing, to thoughts and feelings of injustice and rage, which we know is not the state of mind to be in to perform at our best.

Imagine going for a job interview when you're mad at the interviewer, or cooking a meal for guests who have put you in a foul mood. Imagine standing in the tee at a par-four over water when you're mad at your opponent for not conceding a putt (that you subsequently missed) on the previous hole. We are not going to be at our best, and will probably perform below our true abilities.

In all these situations the focus is in the wrong place: on the anger. This only draws attention to it, and the feeling will linger rather than go away. We have to **focus on outcomes we want and are able to influence, and not events that are in the past and cannot be changed.** Some players allow themselves to vent their anger, through an on-course anger management system, which they use to defuse their frustration quickly. It is worth thinking about a routine to help drop the rot that is anger on the course.

Visualisation exercises can help a great deal. We need to imagine ourselves in a situation where we would normally get angry, but rather than giving in to anger we instead envisage ourselves staying calm and relaxed, even smiling (see exercise 3 Manage the Heat). To have a real effect such visualisation exercises require regular practice. Other methods can help: taking two or three slow deep breaths, focusing on both the inhale and the exhale, creates a physical release of tension and stress. Making a conscious choice to think of something positive distracts us from the negative feelings associated with anger.

Bobby Jones said, 'Golf is a game played one shot at a time, but it took me many years to figure that out.' As clichéd as this may sound, it is clichéd because it finds its origin in truth. Our focus should never be on the last shot, it should always be on the next shot.

A good way to put this insight into practice is to orient our attention towards the outcomes we want and think positively. If we are playing in a match and have just hit a bad shot or lost the hole through poor play, there is little to be gained from getting mad due to the frustration or embarrassment you may have experienced. Rather, analyse what caused the poor shot and make a mental note of how to approach a similar shot when it recurs.

Positive thinking – and focusing on desired outcomes – can be better developed by practising visualisation exercises regularly, so that, with time, playing 'one shot at a time' and not dwelling on past mistakes becomes automatic. This allows us to be more calm and relaxed when something goes wrong on the course. It also allows us to recover much more quickly from any frustrations that do occur whilst playing – as they inevitably will.

Getting mad is a waste of time, breath and energy; choosing instead to stay positive, calm and focused will re-channel these resources to a more productive end. In the 1940s and 50s there was a well-known US golfer who was as famous for his bad temper on the course as for his US Open win in 1958. He was known to break clubs during a round and throw them into lakes and trees; his temper was legendary and he was known as 'Thunder' and 'Terrible Tommy'. He once said, 'Always throw your clubs ahead of you. That way you don't have to waste energy going back to pick them up.' However entertaining it may have been for the spectators, such histrionics were no good for the game: they led to the introduction of a rule prohibiting such behaviour. This player was inducted into the Golf Hall of Fame, but it is thought that his temper cost him more wins than he would care to have admitted. Later in his life he confessed that he regretted being known for his club-throwing and on-course temper, and said that after a while it had become expected of him and so turned into showmanship. Ben Hogan said of him, 'If you could've screwed another head on his shoulders, Tommy Bolt could have been the greatest who ever played.' If evidence is needed that losing your temper is a waste of energy and opportunity, this comment of Hogan's provides it.

The research on success indicates that people who have a positive (happy, joyful, optimistic) state of mind are more likely to succeed than those who have a negative (angry, miserable, depressed) attitude. These findings, which are the result of over 200 studies[1] involving over 275,000 people, demonstrate that negative people look outside of themselves to events and achievements as landmarks of their accomplishments in order to make themselves happy. Positive people, on the other hand, do not make their good feelings conditional upon outside events and achievements. They live free of the fears and stresses that hold back those negative and angry individuals.

I think this goes some way to explaining those amazing birdie streaks that we read about from the professional tour, those occasions on which a golfer plays the most consistently wonderful golf. I would take a big bet that none of these players do this when they are angry, fearful or negative. They are not telling themselves, 'I will only be happy if I make another birdie.' They are thoroughly enjoying the experience, because they are playing in a positive or neutral state of mind.

Such a streak ends more often than not when the player becomes aware of how well they are scoring and starts *trying* – as opposed to just allowing the experience to flow. I have repeatedly stressed the importance of positive thoughts, emotions and attitude on the golf course. This is because, irrespective of how we are playing, such an attitude puts us in the best place to manage pressure and recover from setbacks.

1   Lyobomirsky S, King L & Diener E (2005) 'The benefits of frequent positive effect: does happiness lead to success?' *Psychological Bulletin 131*, 803–55

Golf is a game of control, not only of the swing but also of the emotional state that best serves us when we are under pressure. I very much doubt that getting mad ever won the day.

23
NEVER PLAY THE BLAME GAME

'A man can fail many times, but he isn't a failure until he begins to blame someone else.'

John Burroughs

Do you have a sporting hero? Someone you admire for the way they play the game, who is gracious in both victory and defeat, who exemplifies the spirit of the game they play and provides a role model for others. We choose our heroes as they reflect an ideal to which we aspire. But more than anything else, and almost without exception, the one thing all our heroes have in common is that they are winners.

I do not believe these players are our heroes *because* they are winners (though that is what may have attracted us to them in the first place). They are our heroes because of the strong qualities of courage, patience, dignity and stoicism that make them appear strong. In the 1970s Björn Borg won Wimbledon five times in a row. When he played he rarely smiled, never argued with the umpire, even if the calls seemed unfair, and never lost his temper or smashed his racket. In his sixth consecutive Wimbledon final, in a nail-biting tiebreak for the championship with the talented but volatile John McEnroe, Borg's expression never changed – it remained impassive and strong throughout. One likes to imagine such players are beyond the human emotions of panic and choking. But I am sure Björn Borg felt all those emotions that day as he faced McEnroe.

The reason I mention Borg, a tennis player instead of a golfer, is because I consider him to be mentally the toughest sportsman I ever saw. Under the spotlight of grand slam finals, with nowhere to hide and no one to blame, he exemplified the ideal of being 'strong under pressure'. He won eleven of the twenty-seven grand slam events he played in, giving him a 41 per cent winning average for those tournaments, which is quite phenomenal. However, the fact he retired at twenty-six years of age suggests that the pressure took its toll. The same could be said of Bobby Jones, who retired at the age of twenty-eight, having won thirteen majors (both the British and US amateur championships were considered majors).

There are players in golf who are mentally tough, because of their genetic make-up, their upbringing or particular life experiences. These are the players who will be the last to choke, as their attention is focused on winning and playing well when under pressure. But we should not assume that they do not feel pressure, that somehow they are immune to it. On the contrary, such players have just learned to manage it, or in some cases overcome it. And we should learn from them: when they experience bad luck they rarely argue with a referee, or get mad when things start to go wrong.

It is easy to blame circumstances or people for the misfortunes that come our way. We can blame the caddie for a bad club selection or the greenkeeper for not doing a good job cutting the grass. We can blame the weatherman for giving us a bad indication of the wind strength, or the tournament committee for putting the pins in such ridiculous positions. We can blame our golf teacher for not helping us become better. We can blame our partner for the fact they're wearing a red sweater. We can blame just about anyone and anything we can think of because we are unwilling to accept that we may be at fault. **If we hit a bad shot** we need to accept that it's our fault, but we shouldn't continue to beat ourselves up about it. Rather, like the players we admire, **we should accept it without judgement, and move on.**

I spoke to a young player once who told me he was sure he would have been a better golfer if his parents had given him more opportunities to play and practise when he was younger. I could have mentioned many of the great golfers who came from poverty, were self-taught, and went on to win majors, but I doubted very much this young player would listen to what I had to say. He had become locked into the view that his situation was the fault of others. He had allowed himself to focus on things he couldn't change, rather than orient his thinking toward his personal golfing goals and put himself in the right mental state to go after them. One of the keys to being a good player under pressure is the overwhelming, at times obsessive, desire to win, to compete and play well and to stay in control. We cannot harness this desire if we are constantly on the lookout for an excuse to explain why we failed to play well.

Seve Ballesteros was a self-taught golfer who famously began playing golf on the beach hitting pebbles with an old three-iron. He had all the ready-made excuses he required if he didn't become a good golfer, but his overwhelming desire to win took him to the very top of the game. In the latter part of his career, when he was no longer winning, he began blaming his caddie or the conditions to explain away his poor play. He tried many different approaches and sought advice from many playing colleagues, in search of a way to restore his game to its former glory. One of the challenges we face in golf and in life is to accept the things that don't go our way. This can be seen in Björn Borg's approach, as well as that of Bobby Jones. They both appeared to accept the bounce of the game, both good and bad. This is not to suggest it didn't bother them, but they knew how to let it go, and get on with the shot in hand. This is possible when we trust in our ability, and believe that we can overcome any setback and win.

It is hard for champions as they get older to accept the limitations of age and ability, but wisdom comes from knowing when to put it all into perspective, as well as how to let go of a 'victim' mentality and choose a positive measured outlook. When we start to blame circumstances through negative speech and negative thinking, we will only deepen our sense of 'victimhood': such thinking will entrench our worst behaviours and exert a destructive influence on our actions. Remember, attitude influences thinking, and thinking influences actions. Blaming other people or events on the course will not make them go away. In fact, **the more we complain and blame, the more negatively we think and behave and the more poorly we perform.** In extreme cases, negativity can cause us to lose focus completely and succumb to a meltdown.

Naturally, there will be times when we feel justified indulging in the blame game. When someone talks during our backswing, or stands in our line of sight, or forgets to put their cell phone on silent, we are justifiably irritated. But there is something we can do about such things: we can ask them to move, stay quiet or switch their phone to silent. If someone is at fault, pointing it out is not a bad thing to do; better they know than we suffer poor form. Nevertheless, the majority of the things that bother us are things over which we have no control – a gust of wind, a bad bounce, a car backfiring, or a butterfly flapping its wings too loudly in a neighbouring field. And the things we cannot control should not occupy our energy, because we have something more important to focus on – our next shot.

Staying calm and just 'letting it go',
irrespective of the unfairness of it,
will serve us better than feeling
victimised and distracting ourselves
from the task of playing our best.

24

NO NEED TO PANIC

'Of all the hazards, fear is the worst.'

Sam Snead

There are few worse feelings in life than that of panic. When we arrive at the airport just in time to make a flight, and discover we have left our passport in the hotel room. When we inexplicably oversleep the morning of an important meeting. These are moments of helplessness, when everything seems to be going against us and we feel it's too late to do anything about it. Our mouths go dry, our hearts race, and we feel an emptiness in the pits of our stomachs. We all know that feeling: panic occurs when we are overwhelmed by a situation and do not know what we can do to resolve it.

The dictionary definition of panic is 'a sudden uncontrollable fear or anxiety, often causing wildly unthinking behavior', which is a very good description of the thought process we can experience when we have a panic on the golf course. We never experience panic on the golf course when we are winning, only when we are losing, or when the game is slipping away from us. Sometimes one bad shot is all it takes, one lapse in concentration, to sow the seed of doubt in us. It is choking in its purest form, and at its worst mild tension gives way to full-blown loss of control.

I remember playing a competition at Prestwick Golf Club in Scotland (site of the first Open Championship in 1860), in a four-ball better ball match that was part of a team event. My partner, David, and I were very much the underdogs, as we were playing the opposing team's two best players, and to make matters worse I had lost badly in my morning matches, courtesy of a wild hook (after years of fading the ball off the tee).

I remember our feeling very much like lambs going to the slaughter, and the looks we got from our fellow team members suggested they felt the same! We halved the first two holes, and on the third David holed a bunker shot for a very unexpected but most welcome birdie. On the fourth hole I sank a putt from 25 yards off the green, and so surprised was I that I actually apologised to my opponents. Our opponents now started making mistakes, which I can only assume was due to the fact they were feeling the pressure in a match they had expected to win comfortably. More through good fortune than talent, we remained all square until the ninth hole, where once again a huge putt fell for a birdie and we were three up after nine.

My partner and I were still a long way from a win, and had work to do; we did not discuss the score, but simply concentrated on playing the next holes well. This obviously did the trick as we then won the tenth and eleventh, and found ourselves five up with seven to play. As we walked onto the twelfth tee, I am sure we both had the same thought. Nothing was said, but we knew it would be truly disastrous if we were to lose this match. But it was still possible to lose. We had been fortunate in winning a number of holes unexpectedly, but we knew both of our competitors to be tough players who were still far from beaten.

Just one negative thought. That's all it takes. Just one moment of uncertainty and doubt and we open the floodgates on our confidence and self-belief and let them drain away. My partner David and I had let in a negative thought (and we later admitted to having the same thought at the same time): to lose this match now would be a disaster.

As the pressure to close the match out and win increased, so too did the pressure we felt from our opponents. They, on the other hand, had no pressure given the state of the match, and were relaxed. They began to play the golf we knew they were capable of. They both fired their drives up the twelfth hole with the precision of a short-range rifle shot and made comfortable pars. At the thirteenth one of them made a birdie; at the fourteenth they both made textbook par. Meanwhile my partner and I struggled simply to make a good swing at the ball. We had effortlessly lost three holes in a row and were now only two up with four to play. The fifteenth was the hole when we both entered the panic zone. Not only were the wheels coming off, but, if further proof were needed of our disastrous collapse, we managed to lose to a bogey. Now we were down to one up with three to play. Yikes!

I am sure many of you are familiar with this dynamic on a golf course, when a large lead is frittered away and there is seemingly nothing we can do about it. It happens when we focus on not losing rather than the next shot we have to play; we are not in the present, we're in the future; our attention is not on victory but on defeat. This is negative thinking at its most destructive, and, as is often the case, it is usually triggered by one simple negative thought: the image of a painful outcome we had not previously given much consideration.

On the sixteenth tee, our opponents' tails were well and truly up, and they both hit superb drives that split the fairway. By contrast, my partner hit his worst drive of the day, which scampered like a scared rabbit into some rough eighty yards left off the tee, and I pushed my drive right into light rough. We gave each other a rather fatalistic shrug of the shoulders and went to find our balls, aware that very soon we would be all square with just two holes to go and the final outcome of the match more or less a foregone conclusion.

My partner found his ball and hit it down the fairway. I found my ball sitting in light rough on the right side of the fairway. As I looked to see where our opponents were, I could see them both shaking their heads and looking at the yardage charts. They had both landed in the same bunker. It was not visible from the tee box, but rather than having a short iron to the green, they were both up against the face of a pot bunker with no option other than to play out sideways. I hit a seven-iron that just stayed above ground, a few feet off the putting surface. Then, after my opponents both hit the green with their third shots, I was able to two-putt (more by chance than design I can promise you). We went two up and halved the seventeenth, so managed to record a two & one victory.

In my opinion, panic and choking are based on the same causes. The difference is, we can create strategies to recover our composure when we feel ourselves choking, but panic is more challenging – we need to nip it in the bud as quickly as possible. In the case of the four-ball match described above, my partner and I were unable to stop ourselves thinking that we were going to lose, and this was because we thought we had been lucky and that our luck had run out. Had our partners not gone into the bunker at the sixteenth, we would almost certainly have continued to play in a cold sweat.

We need a strategy to manage panic on the course. I believe that creating a physical and mental pre-shot routine is one of the best ways to do this. It allows us to get into a familiar space where we can switch off conscious thought and play automatically and instinctively.

When we find ourselves on the course and the panic begins to build, we must take control of our breathing and stop thinking negatively, remind ourselves that we are still in the game, that all is not lost. We should use encouraging language about ourselves and our partners. Negative thoughts are just thoughts, not facts. They are our imaginations rehearsing possible 'bad' scenarios in our mind's eye. Why would we rehearse such outcomes? We should not linger on them, or think that they are in some way real; we must refuse to accept that things are going to end badly.

> **The more we practise managing stress on the course, and through visualisation exercises at home, the easier we will manage it – both in competition and life.**

25

MAKE GOOD CHOICES

**'In golf, finally, it all gets down to the player,
the club and the ball, and no other people.'**

Peter Alliss

When the oil billionaire John Paul Getty, at that point the richest man in the world, was asked by a young journalist for the secret of his success, Getty paused for a moment, then said, 'Son: three things. You might want to write them down.' Thinking he was about to get the scoop of a lifetime, the young journalist got his notepad out.

'One: get up early.' The journalist wrote this down as though he was Moses receiving the Ten Commandments.

'Two: get up early.' Now, the journalist was no idiot, and began to think this wasn't quite the exclusive scoop he had hoped for. Finally, standing up and after a dramatic pause for effect, Getty proclaimed:

'And number three is strike oil!'

Sometimes the best advice is the most obvious, but also the furthest from our immediate grasp. 'Make good choices on the golf course' seems such an obvious piece of advice as to seem like no advice at all. Yet I have seen mid-handicap players take on high-risk shots, which were at best a hundred to one on being successfully executed. Rather than lay up and accept a bogey, they convince themselves that they can make it, more in hope than expectation. Almost without fail, they get themselves deeper into trouble, all because their ego gets in the way of an honest and realistic assessment of what needs to be done to avert disaster.

One of the best examples of not making good choices was seen in the 1999 Open Championship at Carnoustie in Scotland. This championship is remembered not for Paul Lawrie's victory, but for the spectacular loss of the tournament on the very last hole by the French golfer Jean Van De Velde.

Van De Velde was a good journeyman pro who had never won on the tour, but during that week in Carnoustie he played near-flawless golf, and when he came to the final hole on the last day he had a three-shot lead over the field. The historical significance of the occasion was not lost on the commentators, who announced he would be the first Frenchman to win the Open Championship since 1907. He was in that enviable position of being able to take a double bogey on the last hole and still win the tournament. Fellow professionals, journalists, experts, caddies and armchair spectators all had their own view on how he should play this last hole. The eighteenth at Carnoustie is a treacherous finishing hole with a burn (a small stream) that crosses the fairway at two points. It is a hole you would expect a professional golfer in this position to play conservatively, cautiously taking an iron off the tee, just to be on the safe side.

What happened on that day in 1999 has assured Jean Van De Velde his place in golfing history, because he took a triple bogey on the last hole, and subsequently lost in a play-off to Paul Lawrie. Much has been written about that fateful hole. I have read and watched interviews with the other players and Jean himself, and of one thing I am sure: Jean Van De Velde did not choke. He made bad choices. He didn't put himself in the best position to win, because his choices were bad. He failed to take the easy or safe option.

On the eighteenth tee he should have taken an iron, which would have made it impossible for him to drive into the burn. But with Gallic gusto Van De Velde elected to take his driver. He had been hitting it well all day, and with a rushed tempo hit a push off the tee that faded to the right and yet somehow miraculously stayed above ground and did not go into the dreaded burn. When I watch the video footage of this tee shot I delight in the fact that after hitting the drive and seeing it remain out of the burn, he smiles and gives the spectators a wonderful 'That's life' shrug of the shoulders.

As we were soon to discover, for whatever reason, at this point the golfing gods stopped smiling on him. He could easily have hit the green with two wedge shots. A friend of mine was watching the tournament live on television in a bar in St Andrews, with a group of old experienced caddies, who were shouting at the caddie on the screen, 'Give him the wedge!' But Jean wasn't listening to the caddies in the Whey Pat Tavern in St Andrews that day; in fact he wasn't listening to his caddy either who, unlike other more experienced caddies, lacked the confidence or experience to tell his player what to do. Jean Van De Velde decided he would hit his two-iron, his rationale being it would get the ball very close to the green and if it went into any of the spectator stands he would get a free drop.

He pushed the two-iron to the right, and it went towards the spectator stand on the right-hand side of the fairway. What happened next was a one-in-10,000 event: his ball struck the one small piece of the stand that, rather than ricochet it forwards upwards or sideways, bounced it directly backwards about fifty yards into deep rough on the wrong side of the burn.

The rough at that year's Open was particularly penal, and Jean had the choice of coming out sideways or going for the green. He opted for the more unforgiving option and his shot to the green, hit without any power due to the thickness of the rough, went straight into the burn, fifty yards ahead. With the ball in the water, Jean then caused a sensation by electing to play the ball from the burn. This remains for me one of the most painful things I have ever watched on television: I felt as though I was watching a man's career implode. Without realising it, Van De Velde was committing career suicide in front of an audience of hundreds of millions around the world. Finally, as the reality of his situation came into focus, he elected to take a drop. He now needed to get up and down in two shots to win. He chipped into a greenside bunker and then splashed out and sank a brave seven-foot putt to get himself in the play-off. But the tension and mental drama he had experienced suggested his Open was lost, and in the play-off he did not feature as a possible winner.

In interviews afterwards Jean Van De Velde defended his decisions and the logic that informed his choices. He was very stoic and philosophical about the whole fiasco, and added that in the final analysis he concluded it was only a game – a sentiment, I may add, that was not shared by many of his professional colleagues; Jack Nicklaus said, 'It wasn't only a game, it was the Open Championship for goodness sake.'

At no time did Jean Van De Velde hit a terrible shot. He didn't hit good shots, but they weren't mis-hits; rather he pushed his drive then he pushed a long iron – quite understandably in the circumstances. But they were not the smart option. He should not have played a driver off the tee, or hit a two-iron for his second shot. The ricochet off the grandstand and the horrible lie in the rough were random occurrences, and even in the burn the ball was sitting on some mud, with half of the ball above the water. By the play-off, he was an emotionally spent force, shell-shocked by what had just happened.

After the tournament, Van De Velde continued to play on the tour and, from interviews he has given, it does not appear the experience broke him as a golfer. I am sure he regrets the decisions he made, but

I have never heard him say he would play the hole differently if he got the chance. He did fire his caddie some time later, but I imagine that was no surprise given the circumstances.

The key lesson we can take from this is that **when we are in a position to win, we must do what it takes to win by the safest and most sensible route available.** We must keep our brains engaged and think clearly and strategically, especially when the pressure is on.

People will continue to remember this extraordinary final hole of the Open Championship for many years. I have heard commentators say that Jean had lost his mind, or seemed to be wholly unaware of the importance of the situation. I don't think either of those sentiments is true; I think he got himself into a position to win, but made bad choices.

This is where good course management comes in. In the pro ranks there have been some outstanding course managers, players such as Jack Nicklaus, who was not a death or glory player, taking the tiger line on every hole and trying to hit the pin, but was a conservative player who wanted to stay in contention. Nicklaus believed that if he found himself at the top of the leader board come the final day, less experienced players would try to force a low score and be more likely to make mistakes. So unless the situation required it, he played each hole according to his game plan. Do you have a game plan for each hole? The majority of players are happy to get in on the fairway then onto the green, but **it is worth making a plan for each hole. That way, when we are under pressure, we will not end up second-guessing ourselves, or at a loss as to the best strategy.**

Ben Hogan was another meticulous player who 'walked the course' (often backwards, as he liked to see from the green the best position from which to play in). Bernhard Langer, whose detailed course notes took all the guesswork out of yardages (before the introduction of GPS and laser sights), knew the direction and distance on every shot.

Today such detail is commonplace in the professional game, and though it is an aspect of the game that most amateurs overlook, having a course management plan for each round is nonetheless a very good habit to develop.

When we are in a position to win, we should do what it takes to win by the most sensible route available. That means thinking clearly and strategically.

26

MANAGING THE AGONY

'People don't seem to realise how often you have to come in second in order to finish first … I've never met a winner who hadn't learned how to be a loser.'

Jack Nicklaus

Losing sucks! No one likes to lose; we are conditioned throughout our lives and by nature to want to come out on top. When we come up short, the experience is disappointing and sometimes humiliating. For young children playing games, winning is everything, and when they lose there's often a vocal outburst and sometimes tears and tantrums. As we grow up, experience life and (hopefully) mature, we realise that winning is not everything and losing is part of the game. We learn to accept it, but that does not mean we like it. Accepting things as they are is the best way to let go of them; otherwise we burn negative memories into our subconscious minds, and they stay there and pop up unexpectedly.

Most of us, over time, learn to accept losing. For some people it gives rise to negative emotions, thoughts and feelings. It's okay to be annoyed; it's absolutely natural to be frustrated when we lose a match we really should have won. It is human nature to experience feelings of helplessness and frustration when inexplicably our powers of concentration and control disappear, and we experience failure and loss.

Every golfer who has ever picked up a club and played any form of competitive golf, even at a social level, will have experienced this. There is no magic bullet to take away these feelings. What we must do, however, is recover from them as quickly as possible. But how?

I spoke at a conference in America some years ago. Speaking immediately before me was a skier who had competed in the Paralympics. Her name was Bonnie St John, an African American who, at the age of five, had had her right leg amputated above the knee due to a congenital malformation. She told her life story and how by chance she began skiing, loved it, and pushed herself to get better and better, and eventually found herself many years later picked to represent the USA in the 1984 Winter Paralympics ski team.

After the first of her two competition runs, Bonnie was in the lead on the giant slalom. Over the course of the event, the downhill run had developed a treacherous corner, which had become very icy, and as a consequence the faster racers were falling over. On her second run Bonnie was skiing fast, and at this difficult corner she too fell over. In the time it took her to recover, continue and finish the course, she had gone from the gold medal position to bronze.

When asked afterwards what had happened she said, 'I discovered that the woman who had won also fell at the same corner as I did, and realised that this other woman had simply got up faster than I did.' She added, 'I learned that people fall down, but winners just get up faster.' During her talk at the conference, her message was very clear: winners recover their nerve faster. This is true in sport and in life: the speed at which we recover our composure has a huge impact on our outcomes.

When I was at university studying anatomy and physiology, one of the senior lecturers said that he believed the best indicator to physical fitness was the speed at which we return to a normal resting heart rate after exercise. To put this in a simple context, consider three people climbing two flights of stairs in a building. One is Mr Fit, a seriously competitive triathlete; another is Mr Average, who doesn't do much exercise but is in reasonable condition; the third is Mr Blob, who does no exercise at all, eats all the wrong food in excess, is dangerously overweight and manages his health through medication.

Upon reaching the second floor Mr Fit will probably not even be out of breath and his heart rate will have increased very slightly and likely recover to normal in under two minutes. Mr Average will be breathing harder and feeling the burn in his legs, his heart rate will probably be 60 per cent faster than normal and he will take four to six minutes to recover to his resting rate. Mr Blob will have been the slowest of the three, he will be breathing very heavily and sweating, and his heart rate will have spiked by 80 per cent above normal, and may take up to fifteen minutes to return to normal. We can see clearly in this example that the faster we recover the sooner we are ready to continue at our best.

If we take this notion to the golf course, and apply it to those times when we experience failure and frustration, we can see that we have to let go of the pain of losing a hole or a match, or missing an important shot, and get ourselves back to the state in which we are most comfortable and able to play our best golf.

It would be impossible to pretend that when a twelve-inch putt for victory horseshoes out, it simply doesn't matter and continue on our merry way impervious to the experience we have just suffered. We are human, and we will react emotionally, which is absolutely fine. The key is to let it go as quickly as possible and move on to the next shot.

A good mantra for such occasions is 'Forgive and forget'. It is as true in life as it is on the golf course. If we are unable to forgive others or ourselves for an injustice done to us and hold on to that feeling, it does not improve the quality of our lives. It may give us a feeling of satisfaction, but it will not heal or help us in the long run.

On the golf course, if we carry the agony of a bad shot with us it will bug us and dominate our thinking when we're faced with a similar situation in the future. So if we can simply forgive the feeling of anger and forget the incident then we will be able to move on and give ourselves every opportunity to play at our best.

This is much easier when we become mindful on the course, which means we **keep our attention in the present, looking neither forward nor backwards.** This takes conscious practice: over time it will become automatic, so that when some unfortunate shot occurs we can experience it in the moment, and then quite simply let it go. Not discuss it for the next five minutes; not hark back to it in the locker room when we are adding up our score. It's history: forget it.

Recent advances in positive psychology demonstrate conclusively that we perform better when we are in a happy and positive state of mind. The common-sense notion is that if I win, I'll be happy, and there is a sound logic to that way of thinking: success is our goal; achieving that goal makes us happy. However, it also assumes that our capacity to be happy is conditional, so if winning makes us happy, losing makes us unhappy.

Clinical research highlighted in a book *The Happiness Advantage* by Shawn Achor demonstrates that only 25 per cent of career success is related to intelligence; the remaining 75 per cent is connected to optimism levels, social support and ability to see stress as a challenge and not a threat. The research also shows that the brain is 31 per cent more productive when positive than when negative, neutral or stressed. Happy sales people bring in on average 37 per cent more revenue than those who are not, and happy physicians are 19 per cent better at making a correct diagnosis than those who are negative, neutral or stressed.

If we can make happiness a consequence of how we perceive our world and its events, rather than a product of our experiences and events, we have a powerful tool to employ to our advantage. In the words of the popular song, 'Don't worry, be happy.' When we adopt a positive happy outlook, the things that previously caused us upset and distress are less likely to affect us.

A great place to start is to write down in a performance journal two things that went well and made us feel good about ourselves after every round of golf or practice session. We should add to the journal every time we practise, and in time we will have a journal full of positive self-reinforcement. We will then be more likely to focus on the positives in our game and in time this will become our normal habit and thought pattern.

> **When we fail, it doesn't mean we are failures, it means we *experienced* failure; so we must learn from the experience, accept the outcome, put it into perspective, and learn the lesson.**

27

MAKE YOUR PRACTICE SWING COUNT

'If you are not prepared, somewhere in the quiz there are going to be questions you can't answer.'

Charles Coody

There are certain experiences on the golf course that few players will ever encounter during their lifetimes. Not everyone will enjoy the sensation of a hole-in-one, or imparting backspin with a lob wedge; very few of us will ever enjoy the power rush of hitting a drive over 300 yards, and sadly I am pretty sure none of us will walk through the men's locker room and be universally admired and envied for our ability.

Yet we all have one area of shared experience: hitting a provisional drive. How often have you hit your tee shot so far off line that without hesitation everyone agrees it is lost, and before it has even landed someone says, 'You'd better hit a provisional'? For a golfer, these five words are as close to comforting words as we're likely to hear. We have hit a drive that is so truly awful we don't even bother getting angry, because we're in shock. In contrast, the provisional shot more often than not goes exactly as intended, straight down the middle of the fairway. And the thought pops into our minds, or we say to our playing partners, 'Why couldn't I do that first time?'

Why indeed? Our ease with provisional shots reveals much that can help us improve our mental game.

There are many factors to consider. As we watch our first drive sail deep into the wilds of the rough or the unforgiving lake, a certain pressure is taken off our shoulders – that self-imposed weight of (negative) expectation. This weight of expectation generally occurs when we try too hard, and rather than swing with a natural flowing motion we try to control the ball to the very best of our ability. Paradoxically, this very act of *trying* introduces tension to our swing – the last thing we want. Once the first ball is gone, we relax, and do not waste too much time in hitting the second shot.

When we are under pressure we become more self-aware: more conscious of our surroundings, our thoughts and feelings. As a consequence we try to be more in control than is necessary or normal, and become tense or stressed. Small things that previously we would have ignored now annoy us. On the golf course, anxiety about hitting a bad shot makes as try harder, when what we need to do is focus in on the outcome and relax.

Let's go back to the tee box. We are tense due to the state of the game, and absolutely have to find the middle of the fairway. Under pressure, we attempt to overcome the strain with increased effort, but we find this manifests itself as tension in our movements, rather than a free-flowing, automatic swing. If we were able to hit the first tee shot with the same ease and efficiency with which we hit our provisional tee shots, we would hit a higher percentage of good first drives. If we practise as we intend to play, we will increase the probability that we will play like we practise.

On the tee, **I believe we should make a full practice swing exactly as we wish to strike the ball**. A few gentle waggles to take the tension out of your arms is excellent, but unless we play golf for a living we will not have the consistent quality of strike we would like. Taking a full practice swing over each and every shot can only help. The challenging part is making the strike on the ball that counts in the game, and that is where confidence and commitment come in. If you don't have the confidence to make a committed swing you will almost certainly try to steer the ball off the tee or hit it softly in the hope that it is okay.

Let me give another example that I am sure you are familiar with. We're just off the green and have a delicate chip over a bunker. The ball is in a tight lie, so we have to make clean contact; a delicate shot is called for, requiring soft hands, good touch and finesse. There is no way to putt or bump and run the ball; we have come to our moment of truth on the golf course. We know we cannot drive like the pros, but surely we can chip the ball somewhere onto the green. Out comes the lob wedge and we walk up to the ball, visualise the shot, then take anything between five and fifteen beautiful practice swings, any one of which would do the job admirably. Then we step up to the ball and produce a swing that bears absolutely no resemblance to our practice swing. Most people hit it heavy, or thin it into the bunker, with the odd ball being shanked or sailing over the green as a result of it being bladed. I would argue that our swing has not failed us, because we haven't hit the ball with our swing, we have hit it more in hope than conviction. Our confidence has failed us: at the last moment we have stopped swinging the club as we have practised and simply tried to control the physical aspects of the club head's flight to get it under the ball and create lift.

Too many thoughts, too much self-awareness, all caused by too much tension, lead us to lose confidence and feel. When we hit it heavy into the bunker or thin it over the green, we are never completely surprised or shocked, because we half expected it. We don't plan to lose confidence, just as we believe we really will hit the ball with commitment; it's just that at the very last moment we move from the state of trust to a state of trying. This change is very destructive, not only on the golf course with a delicate chip, but in life in general.

A proper practice swing, which replicates the real swing we want to make, is an excellent part of our pre-shot routine when we experience tension on the course. It helps remove tension from the muscles, and allows us to feel and experience the swing we wish to make. It also slows us down and stops us rushing to hit a shot without thought or attention (the old hit and hope technique). Most professionals take a full practice swing before almost every shot. Applied consistently, visualising the shot we want to make through a practice swing will improve our tee shots and mean we're far less likely to hear the words 'You'd better hit a provisional.'

> **The practice swing should be seen as the opportunity to swing the club with freedom from pressure, exactly the way we plan to play our shot. It will help remove tension from the muscles.**

28

DON'T STOP 'TIL YOU GET TO THE TOP

'Patience and perseverance have a magical effect, before which difficulties disappear and obstacles vanish.'

John Quincy Adams

What is your current golfing ambition? To be better under pressure? To score lower? Win more money at your regular weekend game? Be the best you can be? All of the above? When I speak to the average club golfer, they tell me they want to play better – that's it. I assume this covers all the benefits that come with playing better: lower scores, lower handicap and managing the pressure.

Globally golf is a multi-billion-dollar business. It is therefore easy to assume that the amount that golfers spend on game improvement (lessons, books, DVDs and training aids) is similarly vast. Yet, for all the investment being made in game improvement, I am not sure that the average club golfer is getting better. Golf is and will always be a game played with a club and a ball. Our desire to be the best golfer we can be should not simply depend on game improvement technology, books, professional instruction and gimmicks. As helpful as these all are, they are not enough. We need to take charge of our aspirations and ambitions.

Golfers' garages and back rooms are full of training aids that have been used once and left to gather dust. I wonder how many people have bought an exercise device, having seen it in a well-pitched presentation full of fit folks with perfect abs. Surely, if it can do that for them, it can do it for us too? We buy the product, use it once or twice, don't see any results, find it harder than it looked on the infomercial, and pack it up and store it out of the way. We are showing a natural desire to take a short cut, especially when it comes to being fitter, thinner, better or richer. Golf aids show our desire to be better, but they are exactly that – aids, not magic solutions. I would unhesitatingly say the same about the books I write on golf. They are aids to improvement, but like all aids they only work when we use them.

When we do make improvements, they rarely last. The reason for this is a lack of consistent 'goal focus'. Most people want to get fitter, thinner, faster or richer, but they do not set themselves specific, realistic goals or targets. When I used to go hill climbing in Scotland, my friend would look to the top of the mountain and say, 'There's the target,' and off we would go. We were not on a random wander in the hills for some exercise; we were going to make it up to the peak. When the weather got bad and a mist came down, we would get out the map and compass; if the rain became heavy, we put on the waterproofs. Every obstacle was anticipated so it could be overcome, and unless the weather became so bad that it was dangerous to continue, we always made it to the top. That was our goal. On one or two occasions it was very hard going, the two of us struggling with heavy packs and a steep final ascent which made our legs and lungs feel as though they were on fire. But my friend Andy would repeat a short and simple mantra, 'Don't stop 'til you get to the top', over and over again – and we didn't.

His logic was that a five-minute rest stop soon became fifteen, and getting restarted when you were tired was harder than it was to keep going. He told me on every step, 'Gain some altitude.' Even if it was only a few inches, it was a few inches closer to the summit.

Once when I was very exhausted, I realised I had slowed down to a rather sad shuffle, with the summit some five hundred feet above me. I looked up and saw a bush thirty yards ahead, and that became my goal: get to the bush. As I got to the bush, I fixed upon a small boulder as my next destination, and then a clump of grass. I broke the journey to the summit into a series of smaller, manageable goals, and suddenly there was the summit.

I believe we golfers always need to have goals. Goals that inspire us and are both realistic and long-term. Saying, 'I am going to halve my handicap in the next year' is ambitious, but is it really realistic for most of us? How many golfers manage to halve their handicap in a year? Not many, and I think the reason is that they regard the goal as being unrealistic, and consequently don't commit to it fully.

Weight loss is another example. How often, around New Year, do we hear people announce, 'I'm going to lose a ton of weight, start going to the gym and get fit'? They all mean it, and even believe it too! But the goal is unrealistic, and progress towards it feels too slow. We need to break our big, ambitious goals down into smaller goals first, to give ourselves the chance for positive reinforcement and celebration.

If you want to get your handicap down from sixteen to eight, the first step in that journey is to get down to fifteen. Then you can think about fourteen. Just as, in the final push for the summit of the mountain, my five hundred feet was broken down into a series of mini-goals each about thirty yards apart, until my final mini-goal was the summit itself. Weight-loss happens one pound at a time; golf improves one stroke at a time.

If we set positive long-term targets for ourselves and put in meaningful, goal-oriented and result-driven practice, we will move forward and improve. It will make us much more aware of what we need to do to improve. This all builds confidence, which we take onto the course, and this confidence is the basis of managing pressure.

Just as most hill walkers take a map and compass, to chart progress and make sure they are going in the right direction, it is a good idea to create a notebook in which to write our goals and chart our results on every round and practice session, making notes of what worked and didn't. This allows us to become aware of the changes we are making; it makes us more responsible with our practice; and it can even make interesting reading.

I only suggest this tactic to serious golfers, those who want to play their best possible golf. Those who are able and willing to put in the dedicated practice that is available to professionals or full-time amateurs. It is a big commitment and the reason why so few average players are able to halve their handicaps in a year.

> **Whatever goal we set ourselves, we need to break it down into many smaller, manageable goals. As each one is achieved, our confidence will grow, and so will our pressure threshold.**

29

PREPARE FOR SUCCESS

**'Most golfers prepare for disaster.
Good golfers prepare for success.'**

Bob Toski

Do you expect to win, or do you hope to win? The majority of club golfers and many pros would say they believe they can win and hope they do. But **hoping is too passive a state of mind to be in if we really want to win; we need to** *believe* **we can win**, and act in accordance with that belief. If we just 'hope' we are going to win, we are accepting that our success is out of our hands. Golf is not a lottery: winners truly believe they can win; they don't keep their fingers crossed in the hope that things go their way.

There is a story from ancient times of a farmer with two young sons. After his wife died suddenly, the farmer had two young boys to raise, a farm to run by himself and no companion to help him. He toiled as best he could to support the three of them, but over the years became embittered. He felt betrayed by life and the hardship of bringing up two boys alone, and no longer trusted anyone. When the older of the two boys was sixteen and the father could no longer support him, he left home to make his way in the world. His father took him aside, gave him a little money and the following advice: 'Son, it is a cruel world out there. Never trust anyone, because they will let you down. The world is full of crooks looking to steal your money, so look after yourself first. Be careful and good luck.'

With the passage of years the farmer gradually mellowed and became more relaxed about life in general. When the younger son reached the age of sixteen, he too decided to leave home and seek his destiny. As he walked his son to the door, the farmer gave him a little money and said the following advice: 'Never be afraid to help others as you go along, because the more you give, the more you get in return. Open your heart to life and let others in. If they let you down, forgive and forget, and do your best.' In short, the opposite of the advice he had given to his older brother.

Some thirty years later the father died and the sons returned for the funeral, and they met again. When they described their life experiences, they discovered that the world had been exactly as their father had described it.

Though this is an old fable, it makes the point that we see and experience what we expect. Psychologists know that if we think something bad is going to happen in the future we look for the evidence to validate that belief, and as soon as something fits our expectations we immediately think, 'I was right.' This works the other way too: if we believe something good is going to happen, we will look for the evidence of that expectation. **Believing we will win does not mean we will win; it means that whatever happens we will stay focused on winning, stay positive and minimise the impact of negative 'stuff' around us.**

In the 2010 Ryder Cup, played at Celtic Manor in Wales, torrential rain caused play to be abandoned on the first day and consequently led to the singles matches being played on the Monday, instead of the Sunday. By the end of the second day the score was Europe 9½ vs USA 6½. This meant that to win the Ryder Cup Europe had to win five of the singles matches, while the USA had to win seven and a half points to retain the trophy. The Europeans know that the American players often do better in the singles than the Europeans, so the pressure on every singles match was immense, and history was in the USA's favour.

Walking to the first tee, the European player Ian Poulter was asked by a television commentator how he felt he was going to get on. The ever-confident Poulter said without hesitation, 'I'll deliver a point.' The interviewer remarked that anything could happen out there, and asked Poulter if he was sure. Without any arrogance or irony, Poulter said again, more firmly and forcefully than before, 'I'll deliver a point.' He went out and played superbly, shot after shot and putt after putt finding the target, and he beat Matt Kucher five and four. Poulter believed he would win. He did not second-guess himself. He did not make that statement in hope. There was no *wishing* that Matt Kucher would have a bad day. He expected to win.

We too must **expect to win**.

There are still many variables beyond our control, so believing we are going to win does not mean that we will. But, especially in match play, a rock solid belief that we can win is like an extra club in our bag. It helps us stay grounded when the pressure is on, because the feeling that we can win will allow us to be more relaxed, rather than increasingly tense as we feel control and confidence fade away.

When we are under pressure, we tend to resort to our own way of managing it. I was for many years one of the most negative thinkers on the golf course. I would stand on the first tee in a match and think to myself, 'I hope I don't lose too badly.' I really did think these unhelpful thoughts, and the reason I did so was to protect myself from being disappointed if I lost (this doesn't make much sense now, but at the time it did). This is **one of the problems with negative beliefs: they do not feel negative; they feel normal and therefore we do not question them**, nor do we feel able to change them. But change them we can, and that was my discovery, when I finally understood that the way we think is under our control, and to change our life we need to start with changing the way we think.

To change the way we think is easy, we simply have to adopt a conscious awareness of the impact our thoughts have on us, and question the negative thoughts that creep into our minds. When we find ourselves with a five-foot putt to win, and a negative thought enters our mind – 'I'll probably miss it' or 'Don't push it' – we should ignore that thought, dismiss it. Then we should replace it with a positive thought and expectation; this is easy, but it requires a commitment to a positive pattern of thinking, especially when under pressure.

> **Let's not dwell on what we think we cannot do, rather before every shot let's focus on what we believe we *can* do; always focus on the positive.**

30

A FEW KIND WORDS

**'A word of encouragement during a failure
is worth more than an hour of praise
after success.'**

Anon

If a close friend had just taken a bad fall off a path, and you could see right away they were injured, and from the fright in their eyes that they were obviously afraid that they had hurt themselves, would you say, 'Boy, are you one clumsy chump, well that's what happens when you don't look where you're going!', or would you hold their hand and say, 'You're going to be fine, help is on its way, I got you'?

I imagine you would offer words of comfort and support. You love this friend; they are in pain, injured and afraid. Why would you do anything other than help them to the very best of your ability in both words and actions? In times of crisis, we need reassurance and encouragement to keep our spirits up and our hope alive.

Yet for so many golfers this is exactly the opposite of what they say to themselves when they are out there 'dying' on the golf course. Why are we so cruel to ourselves? We should be kinder. That does not mean we don't care when a shot goes bad; it means that we encourage ourselves to stay positive and keep hope alive. Professional caddies are masters of finding the right words to keep their player focused on the positive and not giving up when the pressure in the heat of battle is at its greatest.

We must not trash-talk ourselves on the golf course, ever. It is a response to feelings of anger articulated inwards, but the message will be more damaging than helpful. When we are quick to criticise our failings and are harsh on ourselves, we reinforce feelings of inadequacy or incompetence, and impose a barrier to positive growth. Such negative self-talk can do lasting damage to our self-esteem.

If we accept that we act in accordance with our beliefs, then confidence will manifest itself in thought, word and action: changes in posture, direct eye contact, clear expectations of success in our minds. This is why we should use kind words, of reassurance and encouragement. Even when things turn out badly, we need to find some positive aspect to take away from the experience.

Too often people use the past as their blueprint for the future. If they have choked under pressure before, they will often carry with them a deep-seated expectation of doing so again. It is better to keep our attention and focus positively in the present – because this is the only place we can do something about our predicament.

When we are under pressure, even in those lonely times when we feel that the wheels are coming off our game, and we are going into meltdown, we really can choose to stay calm, by consciously breathing slowly and deeply plus engaging in positive self-talk with words that are positive and encouraging. Even if we miss a twelve-inch putt to win a match, this is not the end of the world; no one died and nothing bad happened, we just missed a putt. Naturally, we wish we had made the putt, and we will be pretty mad about it for a few seconds – and that's fine. But we have to let go of this feeling of being angry or mad about it, because otherwise we will hang onto it and damage our self-image. The choice is ours.

With few exceptions, the average golfer plays golf to relax and to have fun, but it also figures that the better we play, the greater the enjoyment and fun to be had. So why give in to negative thinking? Why let pressure ruin our enjoyment as well as our game? Conquering the choke point is an opportunity, not just a challenge.

No golf coach in the world would tell someone they are beyond help, or wasting their time. They would encourage them with positive reinforcement and support. We too must encourage ourselves, and this begins by being kind to ourselves on the course. **Don't be your own worst critic. Don't berate yourself. I doubt doing either has made anyone a better or happier golfer.**

Imagine I showed you a drawing by a five-year-old child, and asked you to say three positive things about it to the child when they came into the room. Do you think you would be able to come up with three? I am sure you would. How about, 'I like the drawing,' 'I love the colours,' 'You have a great imagination,' for starters? Likewise, we can always find positive thoughts on the golf course, even in the most stressful of times: we simply need to be aware that positive thoughts will slow the build-up of pressure, minimise the likelihood of having a meltdown and reduce the stress.

Pressure is an integral part of the game in competition. If we are not competing against others, we are competing against ourselves, and that can bring out the best in us – and sometimes the worst. As I keep stressing, it is simply a case of learning to master the pressure; otherwise, as we all know from experience, the pressure will master us. The good news is we really can do it, we can change the way we think, the way we interpret events, and the way we respond to setbacks: all these are within our control. Learning to do it takes time, but investing in our mental development and skill will see a healthy return on the course.

When asked about the shot they most regretted, most golfers – club players, scratch amateurs and professionals – say the one that cost them victory. In each case, the memory of the loss has been burned deeply into their emotional hard-drive. I ask players the same follow-up question: 'Did you hit a good shot?' The majority say they hit a bad shot, and a few say they hit a good shot that came up short or found the hazard.

My advice is always the same: forget it. You can think either that you failed, or that you learnt something. My choice would be to **learn the lesson from every experience of failure**. Just as the child learning to walk, and falling over an average of 240 times, learns through a process of biofeedback how to calibrate its balance and defy gravity, so, as golfers, we have to learn through a process of failure and never give up, always seeking to learn what we need to do to improve.

There is an old Japanese proverb: 'Fall over seven times; get up eight.' Success and winning come to some faster than others, but always through a process of learning and application.

In 2011 Darren Clarke, playing in his 20th Open Championship, won his first major title. He was 42, an age when most professional golfers are considered to be past their prime. Taking a one-shot lead into the final round, he kept his nerve and looked as though he was in control and relaxed. By contrast, 14 years earlier when he was 28 he led the field at the 1997 Open in Troon by 4 shots with 27 holes to go. However bad choices, which he claims were the result of not listening to his caddy, saw that lead surrendered. On the second tee of the final round with a three-iron in his hand Darren hit the first shank of his professional career, the ball ended up on the beach. For a pro whilst in contention for his first major win, surely there can be few more confidence-sapping experiences. It is to his credit that it did not herald a steady decline and catastrophic loss of confidence.

Use positive self-talk to be supportive and encouraging to ourselves, and our partners.

31

COMMIT TO IT

**'Until one is committed, there is hesitancy,
the chance to draw back, always
ineffectiveness.'**

W.H. Murray

The quotation with which I begin this final chapter comes from a Scottish mountaineer who in 1951 led an expedition to the Himalayas to do all the reconnaissance on a route to the summit of Mount Everest. His research and exploration of the mountain laid the foundation for the first successful ascent of the mountain by a British expedition in 1953.

Murray's quote perfectly captures the challenge of playing under pressure, because when we experience pressure induced by fear – we hesitate. More often than not we do this to minimise risk; we try to steer the ball instead of swinging freely and fully as we have done in practice; our putter no longer has a smooth, confident stroke, but is replaced by one that is tentative and uncertain; we lose our feel for the game and in time our confidence too. In life, too, we can see the results of a failure to commit, be it to exercise, diet, relationships, work, or any other area of self-improvement. What we put in is what we get out.

In few sports is this reality more clearly highlighted than golf, for there is nowhere to hide, no one else to blame. It is the player, the ball, the club and the shot to be played. It is up to us and us alone: are we going to rely on luck, or draw on experience? No one apart from the player themselves knows what is going through their mind in the heat of battle, coming down the stretch, be it the US Open or the monthly club medal. Others can hypothesise, indeed writers such as myself can try to imagine what is happening and explain the cause and cure, but it is pure speculation.

Nonetheless there are insights that lift the veil on those players who create magnificence under pressure. In the 1950 Open at Merion, Ben Hogan had to make par on the tough final hole, a long par four. His drive found the middle of the fairway, but he still had over two hundred yards to the green. If you play golf you have probably seen a photo of that shot. Considered the most iconic golf photograph ever taken, of arguably the greatest player of all time (who only eighteen months earlier had just survived a near-fatal automobile accident and spent months in hospital), it shows a golfer in a perfect follow-through position, tracing the flight of the ball, his back to the camera. Imagine the pressure he was under. This was 1950, when steel-shafted forged blades were precision clubs with small sweet spots, and a one-iron (the club he played) left no margin for the slightest error.

Hogan hit a perfect one-iron, reached the green, two-putted for his par, and won the play-off the following day. A private, taciturn man, Hogan gave little away in his rare interviews. However, in his definitive book, *The Modern Fundamentals of the Golf Swing*, Hogan commented on that shot by saying it wasn't inspired or unique, rather he had been practising it since he was twelve years of age. His view was that **the work we do on the practice range prepares us for tournament golf.** The swing we build must be able to stand up to tournament pressure.

We cannot play such shots under even mild pressure if we entertain doubts, because such negative thoughts weaken our confidence, and when our confidence is low, we hesitate. In a game with so many apparent variables the three keys we need to nurture are: sound mechanics (that work for you and you have faith in); confidence (in your ability); and commitment (to every aspect of the shot in hand).

Commitment is something that only we can enact. No amount of instruction or learning can provide it to you. We are not born with it, rather I believe we have to 'self-determine' – to decide to do what it takes to become the best we can be. In Malcolm Gladwell's book *Outliers*, he examines those stand-out individuals in sport and business who rise to the top and stay there, whilst others who seem more talented and more suited to success fall away. He repeatedly mentions the '10,000-hour rule', claiming that the key to success in any field is, to a large extent, a matter of practising a specific task for around 10,000 hours over a relatively short period of time. He cited Bill Gates getting access to the high school computer when he was thirteen years of age, where, over the next few years, he spent 10,000 hours learning to program and experiment. In an interview, Gates admitted that having that time, which others lacked, had helped him succeed. Gladwell also cites the Beatles, who as a young band played 1200 gigs in Hamburg alone, and before they released their first single in 1962, had spent over 10,000 hours playing together.

To put this into context, it would mean twenty hours a week at a specific activity every week for ten years. This capacity to immerse oneself in an activity gives these outstanding figures their perceived talent. I wonder how long it took for Ballesteros, Hogan, Faldo, Player, V.J. Singh and Trevino, players all noted for their work ethic, to reach 10,000 hours?

Other books have been written debunking the myth that winners are 'born', whether genetically gifted, naturally talented or fortuitously into the right social background. There is more. The harsh truth is that it is hard work, a self-determined commitment to being the best, that creates a winner. There is no short cut, but there is room to get better – for all of us. In my first book I mentioned that few people truly invest in really putting in the time to effect the changes they seek. Many practise, but without real purpose; they are mindlessly hitting balls, not learning. They might read a book on sport psychology but they fail to apply it because they are unprepared to take on the daily practice it requires to develop the mind. It could be said they are keen and enthusiastic, but lack, in the final analysis, commitment.

Long-term commitment is the crucial factor in self-improvement. To better ourselves, we must set goals and work towards them. Out on the course, if we want to play our best golf, we have to commit to each and every shot, especially when under pressure, and this requires the confidence that comes from repeated practice and a positive self-belief.

> **There is no room for hesitancy or uncertainty, especially when we are under pressure. It is important to commit fully and confidently to the stroke we intend to make.**

ABOUT THE AUTHOR

Robin Sieger is a bestselling author, motivational speaker and performance coach, with offices in the UK and the USA.

At the age of 29 he was diagnosed with cancer and it was this life-changing experience that made him determined to re-examine his notion of success. He now works as a motivational speaker and success strategist all over the world and his humour and ability to connect emotionally with audiences has made him the first-choice speaker at major conferences for some of the world's most successful companies, including HP, GM, HSBC, IBM, Coca-Cola, Ford, Nokia and Microsoft, where he received the highest ranking of any external speaker.

He is the author of six other books including the international bestseller *Natural Born Winners*, which is sold in over 80 countries worldwide, and *Silent Mind Golf*. He is also the visiting mental game coach at the Concession Golf Club Florida and holds the world record for the coldest round of golf ever played, 18 holes at −26°C in Fairbanks, Alaska on 22 December 2001.

For more information on mental game golf instruction offered by Robin Sieger, please visit www.siegergolf.com or send an e-mail to info@siegergolf.com.

You may write directly to robin@siegergolf.com.

Robin Sieger is based in Sarasota, FL, and Edinburgh, Scotland. He travels internationally delivering keynote motivational presentations to organisations, institutions and companies worldwide. His company, Sieger International, offers a wide range of seminars and educational programmes on peak performance and success to both the public and private sector.

For more information about how to book Robin or Sieger International Trainers please visit www.siegergolf.com.

To enquire about golf instruction for corporate golf outings, private lessons or a keynote talk at a business event, please contact:

In the UK
0845 2305400

In the USA
1 941 313 6859